The 'Scientific Movement' and
Victorian Literature

The 'Scientific Movement' and Victorian Literature

Tess Cosslett

Lecturer in English Literature,
University of Lancaster

THE HARVESTER PRESS • SUSSEX

ST. MARTIN'S PRESS • NEW YORK

First published in Great Britain in 1982 by
THE HARVESTER PRESS LIMITED
Publisher: John Spiers
16 Ship Street, Brighton, Sussex
and in the USA by
ST. MARTIN'S PRESS, INC.
175 Fifth Avenue, New York, N.Y. 10010

© Tess Cosslett, 1982

British Library Cataloguing in Publication Data
Cosslett, Tess
 Science and literature in Victorian England.
 1. English literature—19th century—History
 and criticism
 2. Science in literature
 I. Title
 820.9'356   PR468.S/
 ISBN 0–7108–0302–8

Library of Congress Cataloging in Publication Data
Cosslett, Tess.
 The scientific movement and Victorian literature.
 Includes bibliographical references.
 1. English literature—19th century—History and criticism.
 2. Science in literature.
 3. Literature and science.
 4. Science—Great Britain—History—19th century.
 I. Title.
 PR468.S34C67   1982   820'.9'008   82–10284
 ISBN 0–312–70298–1 (St. Martin's)

Photoset in 11pt. Garamond by Aurophotosetters,
Pondicherry, India
Printed in Great Britain by The Thetford Press Limited,
Thetford, Norfolk

All rights reserved

In memory of my mother
Dr Anna Cosslett

The celebrated Robert Boyle regarded the universe as a machine; Mr Carlyle prefers regarding it as a tree.... . A machine may be defined as an organism with life and direction outside; a tree may be defined as an organism with life and direction within. In the light of these definitions, I close with the conception of Carlyle.... . But the two conceptions are not so much opposed to each other after all... . They equally imply the interdependence and harmonious interaction of parts, and the subordination of the individual powers of the universal organism to the working of the whole.

Never were the harmony and interdependence just referred to so clearly recognised as now. Our insight regarding them is not the vague and general insight to which our fathers had attained, and which, in early times was more frequently affirmed by the synthetic poet than by the scientific man.

John Tyndall, 'Science and Man', 1877

Contents

Acknowledgements

My first thanks must be to Dr Catherine Ing, my supervisor at Oxford, who introduced me to Victorian scientific writing and to Meredith's poetry. Thanks also to Robert Osborn, who first drew my attention to M. Krempe and M. Waldeman in *Frankenstein* ; and to the friends who read sections of the book, gave advice, or just encouraged me to keep writing: Felicity Rosslyn, Russell Keat, David Carroll, Michael Wheeler.

Introduction

It is easy to abstract anti-scientific statements from Victorian literature, and to present a picture of Victorian science as a dreary and dehumanising Mechanism and Materialism which threatened the destruction of Faith or Imagination or Feeling, or all three. According to Tennyson in *In Memoriam*, science wants to prove that we are 'only cunning casts in clay', purely material beings. The poet finds this idea totally repellent:

> Let Science prove we are, and then
> What matters Science unto men,
> At least to me? I would not stay.[1]

Carlyle begins *Sartor Resartus* by ironically celebrating the advances of the 'Torch of Science', by whose means 'it has come about that now, to many a Royal Society, the Creation of a World is little more mysterious than the cooking of a dumpling':[2] science expels Mystery, and reduces Creation to a material process. Matthew Arnold describes science as 'knowledge not put for us into relation with our sense for conduct, our sense for beauty, and touched with emotion by being so put',[3] while poetry, he implies, can effect this necessary relation: science is value-free, emotionless, unpoetic. And of course there are the greedy little grasping Gradgrinds of Dickens' *Hard Times*, with their 'somethingological' studies which have helped to stifle their capacities for Wonder and Love.[4]

In *Science and the Modern World*, A.N. Whitehead actually uses literature as part of his evidence against nineteenth-century science. He presents the Romantic and Victorian poets as isolated champions of a more 'organic' view of the universe, now validated by modern science, but disregarded by the scientists of the time. 'Materialism reigned supreme'[5] he claims. More modern literary critics have largely accepted this picture of Victorian science at odds with literary values. In a recent essay on Tennyson, Robert Langbaum contrasts the relationship between science and literature in the Victorian age, with the celebration of Newtonian physics in eighteenth-century poetry: 'The difference is that for the Victorians, scientific knowledge was antithetical to, rather than productive of, a religious and ethical position.'[6] Similarly, in his introduction to a collection of essays on *Nature and the Victorian Imagination*, U.C. Knoepflmacher laments that 'the imagination of the scientist and the artist never coalesced'[7] in the Victorian era. If Victorian writers do seem to be using scientific conceptions in a more positive way, critics have tended to stress the creative or spiritual force needed to breathe life into such dead and uncongenial abstractions. For instance, Lionel Stevenson, in *Darwin Among the Poets*, begins by assuming that the scientific material 'must be subjected to the processes of emotion and imagination, so that when the original austere ideas of science emerge in poetry they are fantastically masked and robed. A very brief scrutiny, however, reveals the ascetic beneath the mummer's garb'.[8] Here, 'science' and 'poetry' are being presented as necessarily antithetical, very much as in Matthew Arnold's definition.

But if we read the works of the chief Victorian popular writers on science, men like the biologist T.H. Huxley, the physicist John Tyndall, and the mathematician W.K. Clifford, we shall find that there is no such absence of human relevance as in Arnold's definition: science is continually being related to our senses for conduct and beauty, and touched with emotion. Moreover, Huxley and Tyndall continually deny the charge of being 'materialists', they insist passionately that science matters unto men, they demonstrate the importance of Imagination in scientific thought, and they present their view of the universe with a Carlylean sense of Awe and Mystery. These writers can be seen as expressing the values of a Victorian 'scientific culture', sometimes implicitly, sometimes as an explicit substitute for religious belief. And it is the values of science, rather than its practical benefits, that they consider its most important effect. Huxley attacks those who see nothing in science 'but a sort of comfort-grinding machine', for it has 'not only conferred practical benefits on men, but in so doing, has effected a revolution in their conceptions of the universe and of themselves, and has profoundly altered their modes of thinking and their views of right and wrong'. He concludes that 'the real and permanent significance of natural knowledge' lies in its 'great ideas' and its 'ethical spirit'.[9] It is the aim of this book to trace some of those 'great ideas' as they appear both in the scientific writings of the time, and in its other literature.

In 1877, Edward Dowden began an essay on 'The Scientific Movement and Literature' by saying

Any inquiry at the present day into the relations of modern scientific thought with literature must in great part be guided by hints, signs and presages. The time has not yet come when it may be possible to perceive in complete outline the significance of science for the imagination and the emotions of men, but that the significance is large and deep we cannot doubt.[10]

This book does not claim to provide the 'complete outline' that Dowden hoped for, but merely to develop further some of these hints and signs, and suggest the shape that outline might take; there is obviously a great deal more work to be done in this area. As a start, it seems important to look beyond the superficial, explicit anti-scientific statements of imaginative writers, and notice the ways in which the values and the world view of the prevailing scientific culture were nevertheless implicitly assimilated into a wide range of literature. Scientific writers, novelists and poets can all be found putting forward similar views of humanity, society and nature, often by means of similar language and imagery. Of course, the question of 'influence' between science and literature can work both ways: the scientists, being Victorian writers, will most probably be affected by prevailing literary values and styles. Huxley and Tyndall both testify to the enormous influence Carlyle's writings had on their outlook.[11] But it seems less important to worry about in which direction the influence worked than to notice how scientists and imaginative writers are expressing shared values and assumptions.

A good example of one of these shared values is the preference for *gradualism*, as opposed to catastrophism, evolution as opposed to revolution. A. Dwight Culler, in his recent book on Tennyson, points out how pervasive a concept gradualism was in nineteenth-century culture, scientific, political and literary. He notes the coincidence in time between the publication of Lyell's *Principles of Geology* and the passing of the first Reform Bill. Lyell put forward a 'uniformitarian' theory of gradual geological change, in opposition to prevailing 'catastrophist' theories; the Reform Bill represents the country's choice of 'gradualism rather than catastrophism as its mode of effecting political change'. In literature, too, 'to move from the Romantic to the Victorian period is, with many exceptions and qualifications, to move from catastrophism to literary uniformitarianism'. Culler sees 'uniformitarianism' in Tennyson's poetry and George Eliot's novels.[12] This is not just twentieth-century hindsight, Dowden had made the same point in 1877. He contrasts the Victorian, scientific idea of progress with the Romantic idea, specifically as found in Shelley's *Prometheus Unbound*: 'the idea of progress with Shelley was the revolutionary, not the scientific idea.' On the other hand, Tennyson and George Eliot are seen as 'scientific' precisely because of their gradualist, evolutionary concepts of progress:

In English poetry the scientific idea hardly appears earlier than in Mr. Tennyson's writings, and certainly nowhere in English poetry does it obtain a more faithful and impressive rendering ... . The idea of progress, which occupies so large a place in Mr. Tennyson's poetry, is more than non-revolutionary; it is even anti-revolutionary. His imagination dwells with a broad and tranquil pleasure upon whatever is ... continuously energetic within determined bounds.

Similarly, George Eliot's conservatism is seen to have a 'scientific' and evolutionary origin:

George Eliot, in her conception of human progress, is also anti-revolutionary
.... The conservative instincts of George Eliot as an artist have been nourished
by the scientific doctrine with reference to the transmission of an inheritance
accumulating through the generations of mankind.[13]

By singling out Tennyson and George Eliot here, Dowden is
implying that certain writers share the scientific world view,
while others may not. In particular, he contrasts the 'transcendentalism' of Browning's poetry with the more 'scientific'
humanism of Tennyson's.[14] Of course, there are also 'transcendentalist' aspects to Tennyson's poetry, and 'gradualist'
aspects to Browning's, but on the whole I agree with Dowden
here, and this is why Browning does not feature in this book.
Another notable exception is Dickens: by and large, the
Victorian scientific culture I have identified goes along with a
'realist' approach in literature (the opposite holds true today,
when anyone interested in the relationship between science
and literature is usually assumed to be referring to the fantasies
of science fiction). As Stephen Prickett has pointed out in his
recent book *Victorian Fantasy*, Dickens leans more towards a
'counter-tradition' of fantasy, which went against the main-
stream of Victorian realism, and pushed beyond its reductionist
limits.[15] But the conception of ordered limitation is central to
the scientific world view I am interested in here, as I shall
explain. Of course, I am not claiming that all the imaginative
writers who are dealt with in this book are expressing the same
values, or taking over the world view of the scientists in its
entirety. But each writer expresses some important aspect of
that world view, or shares some of its central values.

To illustrate more fully what those central values were, I
want to refer to an incident in Mary Shelley's novel *Frankenstein; or, The Modern Prometheus* (1818) by way of bringing
out further the difference between the Victorian image of
science and that of the preceding Romantic age. As we saw,
both Culler and Dowden contrasted the 'gradualist' approach
of the Victorians with the more 'catastrophist' or 'revolutionary'
attitude of the Romantics. Dowden quotes from Shelley's

Prometheus Unbound to exemplify the Romantic attitude. *Frankenstein* can be seen as exposing the dangers of Romantic Prometheanism, but without providing the compensating Victorian love of gradualism. When Victor Frankenstein arrives as a student at the University of Ingolstadt, he meets two scientists, M. Krempe and M. Waldeman. All Frankenstein's knowledge of science so far has been obtained from out-of-date books of alchemy, which had excited him with their promises of power. M. Krempe, an ugly, unpleasant man, immediately pours scorn on Frankenstein's dreams, and puts him off science entirely. This is how Frankenstein reacts to the meeting:

M. Krempe was a little squat man with a gruff voice and a repulsive countenance; the teacher, therefore, did not prepossess me in favour of his pursuits ... . Besides, I had a contempt for the uses of modern natural philosophy. It was very different when the masters of science sought immortality and power; such views, although futile, were grand; but now the scene was changed. The ambition of the enquirer seemed to limit itself to the annihilation of those views on which my interest in science was chiefly founded. I was required to exchange chimeras of boundless grandeur for realities of little worth.[16]

Krempe seems to represent one pole of the Romantic view of the scientist: the destructive reductionist, who, in Keats' phrase, 'unweaves the rainbow' with his 'Cold Philosophy'.[17] Limitation and reduction are suggested by his very name.

However, Frankenstein has also been recommended to visit M. Waldeman, who lectures on chemistry. M. Waldeman is obviously set up as an antithesis to M. Krempe, the scientist-as-hero as opposed to the scientist-as-villain. His voice is 'sweet', not 'gruff', his lecturing style full of dignity, his manners 'mild and attractive'. His first lecture concludes with a 'panegyric upon modern chemistry', which restores to Frankenstein all his hopes of gaining power and immortality through the pursuit of science:

'The ancient teachers of this science,' said he, 'promised impossibilities and performed nothing. The modern masters promise very little; they know that metals cannot be transmuted and that the elixir of life is a chimera. But these philosophers, whose hands seem only made to dabble in the dirt, and their eyes to pore over the microscope or crucible, have indeed performed miracles ... . They ascend into the heavens; they have discovered how the blood circulates, and the nature of the air we breathe. They have acquired new and almost unlimited powers; they can command the thunders of heaven, mimic the earthquake, and even mock the invisible world with its own shadows.'[18]

This is the seductive voice that sets Frankenstein off on his disastrous Promethean quest for the secret of life: with what monstrous results we all know. But Waldeman, with his grand vision of the scientist's 'almost unlimited powers' over Nature, is presented without criticism here – it is the sort of vision that would appeal to a Romantic age. Krempe obviously represents the dark underside of this vision – his ugliness is reproduced in the ugliness of the monster Frankenstein actually creates. He is the ugly reality that will destroy the dreams of the Romantic imagination, just as Apollonius destroys Lycius's dream in Keats *Lamia*. But we do not admire or thank him for it: he does not seem to be offering a possible alternative. Frankenstein's only alternative would have been to leave science alone entirely, and cultivate the human and domestic sides of his character instead.

But it is the repulsive, restrictive M. Krempe who is transformed by the Victorians into their image of the scientist-as-hero. The Victorian image of science was mostly non-Promethean: the vision is not of man's scientific power ruling Nature, but rather of Nature's scientific laws ruling man. Physically, Nature's 'realities' limit what man can accomplish – there are no 'supernatural' short-cuts; mentally, they limit what he can think – flights of ungrounded, subjective imagination are discouraged. Obviously, Darwin's theory of evolution holds a central place in this image of science. His account of man's natural 'descent' has a humbling, reducing effect on man's pretensions; and his theory is also a link in the chain of scientific explanation by natural as opposed to supernatural causes: science seemed to be progressing towards a unified explanation of all phenomena. This vision can be presented as a dreary and limiting reductionism. But it can also be seen in a more positive light. The all-encompassing laws of Nature have their own order, which has its own beauty if rightly perceived. Instead of being seen as a constricting chain on man's freedom, this order can be seen as a harmonious pattern to which man can adjust and attune his thought and action. First the harsh limitations and realities that Nature presents must be faced, but then freedom can be rediscovered in acceptance of this truth, and effective action in conformity with real possibilities.

A good picture of the ideal Victorian scientist is provided by Tyndall writing on 'The Study of Physics':

The first condition of success is patient industry, an honest receptivity, and a willingness to abandon all preconceived notions, however cherished, if they be found to contradict the truth. Believe me, a self-renunciation which has something lofty in it, and of which the world never hears, is often enacted in the private experience of the true votary of science. And if a man be not capable of this self-renunciation – this loyal surrender of himself to Nature and to fact, he lacks, in my opinion, the first mark of a true philosopher. Thus the earnest prosecutor of science, who does not work with the idea of producing a sensation in the world, who loves the truth better than the transitory blaze of today's fame, who comes to his task with a single eye, finds in that task an indirect means of the highest moral culture.

This culture, Tyndall goes on to say, is 'based upon the natural relations subsisting between Man and the universe of which he forms a part ... . The world was built in order: and to us are trusted the will and power to discern its harmonies, and to make them the lessons of our lives.'[19] M. Krempe here appears transformed and idealised, speaking with the sweet voice of M. Waldeman. This transformation from ugly reductionism to harmonious order is well expressed by Clifford: 'Every time that analysis strips from nature the gilding that we prized, she is forging thereout a new picture more glorious than before.' He goes on to call this 'new picture' a 'new-grown perception of Law'.[20] The idea that the perception of Law has positive as well as negative emotional implications also comes over in Dowden's essay on science and literature:

This conception of a reign of law, amid which and under which we live, affects the emotions in various ways: at times it may cause despondency, but again it will correct this despondency and sustain the heart ... we shall more and more find occasion for joy in the co-operancy of the energies of humanity with those of their giant kindred, light, and motion, and heat, and electricity, and chemical affinity.[21]

'Co-operancy', not Promethean defiance, is the way to joy here. The Promethean image of the scientist of course still exists in the Victorian age, and rises to prominence again in the science fiction of H.G. Wells, where its potentialities for the creation of fantasy are revived. But for the most part it is the transformed M. Krempe who predominates, and I have allowed him to draw the limits of this book.

The approach in each chapter is slightly different: I wanted to avoid stretching all the writers on the Procrustean bed of the same fixed relation to science. I also especially wanted to avoid splitting up the integrity of their works of art in order merely to illustrate parallelisms with the scientific world view. While these parallelisms are pointed out wherever they occur, I am also interested to show how different writers, starting from the ideas, values, images of the scientific writers, create their own more complex and subtle literary structures, expanding the emotional and aesthetic implications of the scientific world view, or dramatising its internal tensions. Thus the chapters on Tennyson and on George Eliot concentrate mainly on one major work of each writer: *In Memoriam*, and *Middlemarch*; the chapter on Meredith focuses on two poems, 'Meditation under Stars' and 'Melampus'; and the chapter on Hardy analyses one long extract from his early novel, *A Pair of Blue Eyes*, and then goes on to trace themes from this passage in three other novels. All four writers I have chosen have some demonstrable biographical connection with and interest in contemporary science, and I touch on this briefly in each of the literary chapters.

The first chapter is devoted to a sketch of the scientific world view as depicted by late Victorian scientific writers. The writers

I have included here can be described as leading scientific naturalists and agnostics – Huxley, Tyndall, Clifford, John Morley, Leslie Stephen. Unlike earlier scientific writers, such as the geologist Hugh Miller, who still wrote in the tradition of Natural Theology, these later exponents of scientific naturalism were concerned to present a coherent and complete scientific world view as a substitute for the existing religious world view. In short, they were engaged in the creation of a myth: and it is the literary reaction to this 'scientific' myth that I am interested in in this book.

These, then, are the main outlines of the area which I wish to explore. To draw attention to the positive ethical and aesthetic implications of Victorian science as they appear in literature, seems to me a more worthwhile and useful approach than to look for more ammunition in the rather sterile and artificial 'battle' of literature against science. Of course there are ways in which science did and does pose a threat to the values of imaginative literature: but one way to defuse this threat is to bring out what is imaginative, human and redeemable within science itself.

CHAPTER 1

The Values of Science

Charles Darwin, as I have suggested, is a central figure in the Victorian image of science. His theory of evolution did not create that image – rather, it fitted in beautifully with the already prevailing trends of naturalism and gradualism. As Tyndall says, 'The strength of the doctrine of Evolution consists, not in an experimental demonstration (for the subject is hardly accessible to this mode of proof) but in its general harmony with scientific thought.'[1] In particular, Darwin fitted in with and carried further the gradualist approach of Lyell – the evolution of life, like geological change, happens by innumerable small changes accumulating over a vast period of time, not by sudden catastrophes or spontaneous creations. So the theory of evolution provides a good focal point for a discussion of the moral and aesthetic implications of Victorian scientific naturalism.

Darwin's theory appears at first rather forbidding and reductive, in the manner of M. Krempe. Man has not been specially created by a benevolent God; he has been inadvertently evolved by an indifferent Nature. His origin is the same as that of animals and plants, and ultimately rocks and stones. The scientific writers see this as a hard truth that has to be faced and accepted, while the easier consolations of the Biblical account of Creation must be rejected. Acceptance of unpleasant truth is one of their central values. But by bringing man himself within the realm of all-inclusive natural causation, Darwin contributes to the unity of the scientific explanation of the world. Huxley pronounces 'the fundamental proposition of Evolution' to be 'that the whole world, living and not living, is the result of the mutual interaction, according to definite laws, of the forces possessed by the molecules of which the primitive nebulosity of the universe was composed'.[2] So here we have again the idea of Law, with its positive connotations of unity and regularity. As Dowden pointed out, the 'conception of a reign of law' offers the opportunity for rejoicing in our 'co-operancy' with our 'kindred' in the rest of Nature.[3] Kinship and co-operation are also implied by Darwin's theory: in *The Origin of Species* he remarks that terms of 'affinity' and 'relationship' formerly used to describe similarities between species, will now cease to be metaphorical, since all are *literally* related in a common 'descent'. Man's 'natural' ancestry can give rise to feelings of belonging and connectedness. The metaphor Darwin chooses to convey this idea of real relationship is the famous one of the 'the great Tree of Life, which fills with its dead and broken branches the crust of the earth, and covers the surface with its ever branching and beautiful ramifications'. Darwin's image of Nature is a living organism, not a dead machine. Organic connection is also implied by the interdependence between species and environment. Darwin remarks on 'the beauty and infinite complexity of the coadaptations between all organic beings, one with another and with their physical conditions of life'.[4] The interconnections take on an aesthetic appeal here; and values of adaptation and co-operation can be implied. Finally, Darwin's theory is an outstanding example of the creative operations of the scientific mind. As Tyndall says in 'The Scientific Use of the Imagination',

In the case of Mr. Darwin, observation, imagination and reason combined have run back with wonderful sagacity and success over a certain length of the line of biological succession. Guided by analogy, in his *Origin of Species* he placed at the root of life a primordial germ.[5]

Tyndall is stressing here the way Darwin's imagination, working by analogy, takes him beyond the observable evidence to the original source of life.

So, to sum up, the main values attached to the theory of evolution were: the acceptance of unpleasant Truth and re-nunciation of 'supernatural' consolations; the vision of uni-fying, all-pervasive Law; the recognition of kinship with Nature; the appreciation of organic interrelatedness and co-operation within Nature; and the admiration for the scientific imagination. I have put them in this order to bring out the idea of an initially unpleasant and limiting reductionism being gra-dually transformed by the recognition of harmony and beauty within the accepted limitations. I want now to illustrate these values one by one in more detail, to fill in our picture of the Victorian scientific world view. After showing the coherence of that world view, I shall then go on to consider some of the contradictions and tensions that are nevertheless implicit in it.

(i) Truth

Tyndall stresses the fearless devotion to truth required by scientific research when he explains how he was first attracted to the subject:

But science soon fascinated me on its own account. To carry it duly and honestly out, moral qualities were incessantly invoked. There was no room allowed for insincerity – no room even for carelessness. The edifice of science had been raised by men who had unswervingly followed the truth as it is in nature; and in doing so had often sacrificed interests which are usually potent in this world.[6]

The editor of Clifford's *Lectures and Essays* similarly finds it important to stress Clifford's dedicated attitude to his work:

This pursuit of knowledge for its own sake, and without even such regard to collateral interests as most people would think a matter of common prudence, was the leading character of Clifford's work throughout his life. The discovery of truth was for him an end in itself, and the proclamation of it, or of whatever seemed to lead to it, a duty of primary and paramount obligation.[7]

For Clifford, the sacrifice was not only of worldly prosperity, but also of profoundly held religious beliefs which he found it deeply painful to part with.[8] Emotional as well as financial rewards must be given up. The danger to truth from self-concerned emotional reactions is explained by Tyndall in defence of the theory of evolution:

Were not man's origin implicated, we should accept without a murmur the derivation of animal and vegetable life from what we call inorganic nature. The conclusion of pure intellect points this way and no other. But this purity is troubled by our interests in this life, and by our hopes and fears regarding the life to come. Reason is traversed by the emotions, anger rising in the weaker heads.[9]

Subjective emotion distorts the picture and obscures the truth – as Tyndall warns, 'We must be careful of projecting into external nature that which belongs to ourselves.'[10]

But this objectivity is not emotionless – it is deeply involved with emotions such as love of scientific truth, and admiration for Nature's independent reliability. Huxley calls himself 'a worshipper of the severe truthfulness of science',[11] and tells how 'Science and her methods gave me a resting-place independent of authority and tradition'.[12] Here the loss of old beliefs is seen as a positive release from constricting traditions, while science offers a new source of stability. Huxley expands this idea in 'The Advisableness of Improving Natural Knowledge', where he speaks of the 'new morality' of scientific advance, which consists in a sceptical refusal to accept beliefs on authority, preferring to test them against 'their primary source, nature ... . Nature will confirm them.'[13] This scientific fidelity to the truth of Nature alone is seen by Huxley as the basis of morality: in 'Science and Morals', he says, 'the foundation of morality is to have done, once and for all, with lying; to give up pretending to believe that for which there is no evidence, and repeating unintelligible propositions about things beyond the possibilities of knowledge.'[14] Clifford too is zealous in this cause: in 'The Ethics of Belief', he argues that it is immoral to guide one's life by beliefs not supported by sufficient evidence, and that belief 'is desecrated when given to unproved and unquestioned statements, for the solace and private pleasure of the believer'.[15] The aim of all this strenuous disillusionment is, in the end, effective action – only by the acceptance of unpleasant truth does this become possible. As Huxley puts it:

there is no alleviation for the sufferings of mankind except veracity of thought and of action, and the resolute facing of the world as it is when the garment of make-believe by which pious hands have hidden its uglier features is stripped off.[16]

The same idea is put more positively by Huxley's fellow agnostic, Leslie Stephen: 'Dreams may be pleasanter for the moment than realities; but happiness must be won by adapting our lives to the realities.'[17]

So the ideal Victorian scientist was seen as heroically rejecting the easy consolations of religion and 'preconceived notions',[18] unselfishly suppressing his personal emotions in order to subordinate himself to the objective truth of Nature, which, in his interpretation, can expressly not offer any personal reward. On the other hand, he could find consolation and support in Nature's reliability as an experimental test of ideas: though the truth may be hard, Nature never lies. She provides a standard of veracity. Acceptance of this standard is in the end the key to effective moral action.

(ii) Law

By openness to truth, the scientist is able to perceive the regularity and order of natural causation operating everywhere. As George Eliot writes in the *Fortnightly Review*:

The great conception of universal regular sequence, without partiality and without caprice – the conception which is the most potent force at work in the modification of our faith, and of the practical form given to our sentiments – could only grow out of that patient watching of external fact, and that silencing of preconceived notions, which are urged upon the mind by the problems of physical science.[19]

Here it is being implied that it is especially moral of the universe to work by natural cause and effect rather than with super-natural 'partiality' and 'caprice'. Tyndall makes the same implication: 'The order and energy of the universe I hold to be inherent, and not imposed from without, the expression of fixed law and not of arbitrary will.'[20] John Morley, the editor of the *Fortnightly Review*, and a leading exponent of the 'scientific culture' I have identified, makes more explicit the moral value of 'fixed law' as opposed to 'arbitrary will':

Why should this conception of a coherent order, free from the arbitrary and presumptuous stamp of certain final causes, be less favourable either to the ethical or the aesthetic side of human nature, than the older conception of the regulation of the great series by a multitude of intrinsically meaningless and purposeless volitions?[21]

Natural causation gives a meaningful and reliable pattern to events – it can provide a dependable 'resting-place', just as scientific truth could, and a basis for faith and morality.

So Huxley sees 'the safety of morality' in 'a real and living belief in that fixed order of nature which sends social disorganisation upon the track of immorality, as surely as it sends physical disease after physical trespasses'.[22] The scientific faith in and search for laws of cause and effect, learnt from Nature, can be applied to the understanding and regulating of human conduct. The consequences of an action, rather than its religious sanction or prohibition, are the test of its morality. In a letter Clifford describes his article on 'The Scientific Basis of Morals' as 'showing that moral maxims are ultimately of the same nature as the maxims of any other craft: if you want to live together successfully, you must do so-and-so.... That responsibility is founded on such order as we can observe, and not upon such disorder as we can conjecture.'[23] The scientific populariser, Edward Clodd, attributes the modern advance in general moral tone to the idea of natural causation:

That heightened tone, which is a yet stronger note of our time, is, in the main, due to the progress of science, using the term as including not merely knowledge of the operations of nature, but knowledge of human life as affected by divers causes ... .

For in proving the unvarying relation between cause and effect in morals as in physics, science gives the clue to the remedy for moral ills.[24]

Edward Dowden, in 'The Scientific Movement and Literature', similarly derives from science a new 'natural rather than a miraculous or traditional foundation for morality',

in the knowledge that consequence pursues consequence with a deadly efficiency far beyond our power of restraining, or even reaching them. The assurance that we live under a reign of natural law enforces upon us with a solemn joy and an abiding fear the truth that what a man soweth, that shall he also reap.[25]

The idea of fixed natural laws, with a price to be paid for disregarding them, is vividly expressed by Huxley in his famous simile of the chess-game:

The chess-board is the world, the pieces are the phenomena of the universe, the rules of the game are what we call the laws of Nature. The player on the other side is hidden from us. We know that his play is always fair, just and patient. But also we know, to our cost, that he never overlooks a mistake, or makes the smallest allowance for ignorance ... one who plays ill is checkmated – without haste, but without remorse.[26]

Again, Nature emerges as a stern but always reliably just Power. Tyndall's image of Nature is less harsh, when he reminds us that the claims of science

are those of the logic of Nature upon the reason of her child – that its disciplines as an agent of culture, are based upon the natural relations subsisting between Man and the universe of which he forms a part ... . The world was built in order: and to us are trusted the will and the power to discern its harmonies, and to make them the lessons of our lives.[27]

Here the natural order is seen not as a harsh system of deadly consequences but as a harmony in which we can co-operate, because we are naturally akin to it.

(iii) Kinship with Nature

The idea of natural causation implies not only dependable regularity but also coherent *unity* in Nature. The tendency of Victorian science was to stress this oneness, by breaking down the barriers between organic and inorganic; Nature is unified by the universal operation of scientific laws; and also by a uniform 'material' composition. This uniformity can be presented as a depressing and ugly triumph of 'mechanism' and 'materialism', driving all 'poetic' beauty from Nature, and finally entrapping man himself in this alien machine. However, this is not the only possible interpretation. Huxley and Tyndall always insist that the new discoveries do not degrade organic life, but rather dignify so-called 'inorganic' matter. Tyndall, in particular, as a physicist, is continually aware of the energies and structural potentialities of 'matter', revealed by discoveries in thermodynamics, for example. So instead of the material analogy being extended upwards, the analogy of life could equally well be extended downwards, and the whole of Nature, including man, be seen as one living organism, rather than one dead machine. Instead of feeling an alien in a hostile universe, man can just as well have a new feeling of kinship with the rest of Nature.

The 'material' bond between man and the rest of Nature is insisted upon by Huxley in his famous lecture 'On the Physical Basis of Life'. His argument centres on researches into the chemical composition of living tissue. Edward Clodd, in his biography of Huxley, gives a good short account of the lecture:

Following on the demonstration of the identical constitution of protoplasm as the raw stuff which builds up the living cell as the structural foundation of every living thing, Huxley showed that the protoplasm itself is built up of certain compounds, and that 'a threefold unity – namely, a unity of power or faculty, a unity of form, and a unity of substantial composition – pervades the whole living world.'

... Each of the four elements of which protoplasm is made up is, by itself, ineffective to produce the organic; united, they are stirred by complex movements of astounding rapidity which constitute the phenomena of life at its simplest; life whose 'hidden bond connects the flower which a girl wears in her hair with the blood that courses through her youthful veins', and the 'brightly coloured lichen, which so nearly resembles a mere mineral encrustation of the bare rock on which it grows, with the painter, to whom it is instinct with beauty, and the botanist, whom it feeds with knowledge'.[28]

Girl and flower, lichen, painter and botanist, are all very literally part of one life. But, as Clodd goes on to point out, Huxley was asserting the kinship not only between all forms of life, but also between life and inorganic matter. Clodd expands this point, referring to researches which demonstrate that the sun, the planets, and even the distant stars, are formed of 'the same stuff' as 'the earth and its living, as well as not-living, contents'.[29] He illustrates this all-embracing identity of living and not-living by quoting Tyndall: 'all our philosophy, all our poetry, all our science, all our art – Plato, Shakespeare, Newton and Raphael – are potential in the fires of the sun.'[30] If we put this statement back into its context, we find that Tyndall presents it as the logical consequence of the theory of evolution: evolutionary theory and researches in physics and chemistry come together here to give this picture of unity.

Edward Dowden brings out the emotional and imaginative implications of this all-pervading unity in his essay on science and literature. Among several 'cosmical ideas of modern science' that for him 'have in themselves an independent value for the imagination', is 'the idea of *ensemble*'. He illustrates this idea by quoting from a lecture by A.J. Ellis:

Everywhere throughout the universe – thus runs the speculation of science – organic or inorganic, lifeless or living, vegetable or animal, intellectual or moral, on earth or in the unknown and glittering worlds we gaze at with awe and delight, there is a consensus of action, an agreement, a oneness.'[31]

John Morley also celebrates 'that great idea of Ensemble throughout the visible universe, which may be called the beginning and fountain of right knowledge'.[32] Dowden insists that this unity with the rest of the universe does not degrade humanity: 'It may be questioned whether man's dignity is not more exalted by conceiving him as part – a real though so small a part – of a great Cosmos, infinitely greater than he, than by placing him as king upon the throne of creation.'[33] Tyndall too is keen not to degrade mankind by his relationship with 'the fires of the sun' – he means instead to elevate matter by showing us its potential: 'had we not better recast our definitions of matter and force, for, if life and thought be the very flower of both, any definition which omits life and thought must be inadequate'.[34] Similarly, in his famous 'Belfast Address', he is led by his belief 'in the continuity of nature' to 'discern in that Matter which we, in our ignorance of its latent powers, and notwithstanding our professed reverence for its Creator, have hitherto covered with opprobrium, the promise and potency of all terrestrial Life'.[35]

Not only does its identity with living matter elevate inorganic matter, but researches in physics and chemistry demonstrate that inorganic matter itself possesses forces and structural powers as mysterious as those of life. Huxley, in 'The Physical Basis of Life', knows he is risking the charge of propounding 'a diabolical materialism', by asserting the unity of organic and inorganic. But he defended himself from this charge, says Clodd,

by the following comparison. the design of which was to show that the ultimate nature of matter is as fully a mystery as that of mind, and that the terms in which we speak of the one are equally applicable to the other.

Carbon, hydrogen, oxygen and nitrogen, when brought together under certain conditions, give rise to the complex stuff, protoplasm, which manifests what is known as life. When two of these elements, oxygen and hydrogen, are mixed in a certain proportion, and an electric spark is passed through them, they disappear, and the result is water. In the one case we talk of a 'vital force' having stirred the dead elements into living matter; but in the other case we do not talk of a something called 'aquosity' having blended the two invisible gases into visible water. Is not the one process as mysterious as the other?[36]

In another lecture, Huxley enthusiastically develops this idea of the 'livingness' of matter:

In nature, nothing is at rest, nothing is amorphous; the simplest particle of that which men in their blindness are pleased to call 'brute matter' is a vast aggregate of molecular mechanisms performing complicated movements of immense rapidity, and sensitively adjusting themselves to every change in the surrounding world. Living matter differs from other matter in degree and not in kind; the microcosm repeats the macrocosm; and one chain of causation connects the nebulous original of suns and planetary systems with the protoplasmic foundation of life and organisation.[37]

Here, both interconnected unity and 'livingness' are stressed, and an aesthetic contrast implied with the conventional concept of 'brute matter'. Tyndall too is moved by the 'livingness' of matter. Writing on ' "Materialism" and Its Opponents', he describes the 'formative power' of matter exhibited in the building up of snow crystals, and its similarity to the processes of organic Nature, and concludes; 'The animal world is, so to say, a distillation through the vegetable world from inorganic nature. From this point of view all three worlds constitute a unity, in which I picture life as immanent everywhere.'[38] So it is possible for man to feel at home as a part of this interlinked universe of living matter.

(iv) Organic interrelation

The unity, interconnection and livingness of the Universe imply that it functions as an organism, rather than as a machine. We have seen how a model of organic interdependence was implied by Darwin's theory of evolution. Tyndall derives a similar image from the theory of the conservation of energy: 'It is as if the body of Nature were alive, the thrill and interchange of its energies resembling those of an organism.'[39] For Tyndall, this concept of organism is central to the physical conception of the universe. He admires Carlyle because

Quite as clearly as the professed physicist he grasped the principle of Continuity, and saw the interdependence of 'parts' in the 'stupendous Whole'. To him the universe was not a Mechanism, but an Organism – each part of it thrilling and responding sympathetically with all the other parts.[40]

The image of universal organism has both aesthetic and moral implications. Aesthetically, the beauty of its interconnected processes can be admired; and a moral lesson can be drawn from the interdependence and co-operation of its 'parts' for the benefit of the 'whole'.

We have already noticed Huxley's aesthetic appreciation of the potentialities of so-called 'brute matter'. In a Note to an essay on Berkeley, he develops this theme further, attacking the 'superstition' that matter is 'not merely inert and perishable, but essentially base and evil-natured'. The example he chooses is a rusty nail, which, when rightly considered, is not a type 'of the passive and the corruptible', but 'an aggregation of millions of particles, moving with inconceivable velocity in a dance of infinite complexity yet perfect measure; harmonic with like performances throughout the solar system'.[41] Nature's 'living-ness' implies universal movement and change, imaged here by metaphors of dance and music, which also convey the idea of 'harmonious' interaction between all the parts of the universal organism. Tyndall also uses musical metaphors to describe Nature's processes. In the Alps he watches snow-crystals forming, and imagines the molecules 'arranging themselves as if they moved to music'.[42] These musical changes characterise not only the 'parts' of Nature, but also the 'stupendous Whole'. In his article 'On the Constitution of the Universe', Tyndall describes the latest results of physical research – the conception of the 'ether', the wave-theory of light, the idea that 'both light and heat are modes of motion', and the theory of the conserva-tion of energy – and concludes:

This, then, is the rhythmic play of nature as regards her forces ... . Thus beats the heart of creation, but without increase or diminution of its total stock of force ... .
   Thus, what is true of the earth, as she swings to and fro in her yearly journey round the sun, is also true of her minutest atom. We have wheels within wheels, and rhythm within rhythm.[43]

   In his book on *Heat*, Tyndall adds to this image of rhythmic change the images of 'waves' and 'flux', suggesting that it is this continuous connected movement that is the permanent reality, rather than physical susbtance. Once again, the imagery is inspired by the conservation of energy,

the law, which reveals immutability in the midst of change, which recognises incessant transference or conversion, but neither final gain nor loss ... . Waves may change into ripples, and ripples into waves, – magnitude may be substituted for number, and number for magnitude, – asteriods may aggregate to suns, suns may resolve themselves into florae and faunae, and florae and faunae melt in air, – the flux of power is eternally the same. It rolls in music through the ages, and all terrestrial energy–the manifestations of life, as well as the display of phenomena, are but the modulations of its rhythm.[44]

All the leading ideas of Victorian science can be seen as contributing to this picture of universal transmutation and insubstantiality. Darwin's theory obviously implies continuous change or 'evolution' in biology – species are not fixed, they are mutable; Lyell shows continuous changes operating in geology – even mountains are eventually mutable; in physics, theories of light and heat suggest that different forms of energy are interconvertible, and that matter itself may be just another manifestation of force. Edward Clodd sums up this picture of universal change within overall unity, again using the image of 'rhythm':

So the changes are rung on evolution and dissolution, on the birth and death of stellar systems – gas to solid, solid to gas, yet never quite the same – mighty rhythmic beats of which the earth's cycles, and the cradles and graves of her children, are minor rhythms.

Thus the keynotes of Evolution are Unity and Continuity. All things are made of the same stuff differently mixed, bound by one force, stirred by one energy in divers forms. Force inheres in matter; Energy acts through it; therefore both have neither more nor less claim to objective reality than matter. And as science tends to the conclusion that all kinds of mater are modifications of one primal element, and that all modes of motion are varied operations of one power, perchance these three – Matter, Force and Energy – are one.[45]

Here, 'mechanism' is not only transformed into 'organism', but 'matter' itself is transmuted away into 'process' – as Huxley puts it:

the state of the cosmos is the expression of a transitory adjustment of contending forces ... . Thus the most obvious attribute of the cosmos is its impermanence. It assumes the aspect not so much of a permanent entity as of a changeful process, in which naught endures save the flow of energy and the rational order which pervades it.[46]

We can see now that the picture of Victorian science that Whitehead presents in *Science and the Modern World* is inadequate: 'the biological developments, the doctrine of energy, and the molecular theories were rapidly undermining the adequacy of the orthodox materialism. But until the close of the century no one drew that conclusion. Materialism reigned supreme.' Whitehead presents his own 'organic' philosophy of science as an entirely new departure. One of its leading ideas is that 'concrete fact is process', 'nature is a structure of evolving processes. The reality is in the process.'[47] As we have seen, Victorian scientific writers had recognised this already.

The concept of universal organism also had moral implications. Though the universal 'process' is more important than its individual 'parts', each part still has an essential effect on the whole. The concept of gradualism stressed this – both Darwin and Lyell drew attention to the cumulative importance of numerous small, insignificant events in bringing about vast changes over a huge time-span. When this idea was transferred to the field of morality, one's most trivial actions took on an awful importance, extending throughout the ages. The sense of the real and momentous effect our individual actions can have on the progress of the race as a whole, present and future, is central to the moral feelings of the scientific writers. Edward Clodd claims that 'Especially is science a preacher of righteousness in making clear the indissoluble unity between all life past, present, and to come.'[48] Clifford insists that 'we are individually responsible for what the human race will be in the future, because every one of our actions goes to determine what the character of the race shall be tomorrow'.[49] Clifford's ideal transcends the deaths of individuals: 'we detach ourselves from the individual body and its actions which accompany our consciousness, to identify ourselves with something wider and greater that shall live when we as units shall have done with living, that shall work on with new hands when we its worn-out limbs have entered into rest.'[50] Here, humanity is being seen as one perpetual, self-renewing organism. Edward Dowden also derives from science a faith that looks through death: 'we have found our deep bond of relationship with all the past, and a vista for hopes, sober but well-assured, has been opened in the future', since 'In the face of death, joy may remain for the individual through sympathy with the advance of his fellows, and in the thought that his deeds will live when he is himself resolved into nothingness.'[51]

(v) Scientific Imagination

It might seem that there was no room left for Imagination in the Victorian scientist's perception of his world. We have seen how he was meant to renounce his subjective feelings in order to achieve an objective picture of the hard truth, the real facts of Nature. The world is governed by the natural law which Reason can recognise, not by the supernatural interventions which have been dreamt up by the Imagination. Of course, the initial choice of Reason over Imagination, objectivity over subjectivity, is in itself a subjective choice, but it is justified by its results. As Tyndall says:

We hold it to be an exercise of reason to explore the meaning of a universe to which we stand in this relation, and the work we have accomplished is the proper commentary on the methods we have pursued. Before these methods were adopted the unbridled imagination roamed through nature, putting in the place of law the figments of superstitious dread.[52]

But 'imagination' here is I think being used in the sense of 'fantasy'. In the same way Leslie Stephen describes a 'scientific' facing of 'reality' in these terms: 'making the best of the materials at our disposal, and conformity to the known conditions of the world around us, instead of the construction of a fanciful palace under the guidance of arbitrary fancy.'[53] The Imagination or Fancy being attacked here is an 'arbitrary', 'unbridled' faculty, dreaming up distorted visions of excessive dread or excessive bliss. But there is another sort of Imagination that works in co-operation with the idea of Law, and that is appropriate and even necessary for the scientist. For the very 'idea' of universal law is a construct of the Imagination, it is not an 'objective' fact or truth, it is the unifying concept that links together a host of otherwise disconnected objective observations. Tyndall contends that without Imagination, the scientific concept of the world would fall apart:

With accurate experiment and observation to work upon, Imagination becomes the architect of physical theory ... . Scientific men fight shy of the word because of its ultra-scientific connotations; but the fact is that without the exercise of this power, our knowledge of nature would be a mere tabulation of co-existences and sequences ... the concept of Force would vanish from our universe; causal relations would disappear, and with them that science which is now binding the parts of nature to an organic whole.[54]

In order to perceive Nature as a unified organism, the scientist must be looking at Nature as a unified organism in the first place. This creative, unifying power of the scientific Imagination is very like the operation of the poetic Imagination as described by Coleridge. Tyndall in fact suggests this:

Never were the harmony and interdependence [of the 'parts' of the universe] ... so clearly recognised as now. Our insight regarding them is not the vague and general insight to which our fathers had attained, and which, in early times, was more frequently affirmed by the synthetic poet than by the scientific man.[55]

It is as if the insights of the poet have now been confirmed experimentally by science. In a review of G.H. Lewes's *Problems of Life and Mind*, Frederic Harrison concludes: 'In a word, our sciences are *verified poems*.'[56]

Like Coleridge's 'Imagination', the scientific Imagination creates organic unity in what it perceives. And it does this by penetrating through surface appearances to an unseen rational order behind them. In Bowra's book on *The Romantic Imagination*, he concludes that the Romantic poets agreed that 'the creative imagination is closely connected with a peculiar insight into an unseen order behind visible things'.[57] This Romantic way of seeing the world appears also in Victorian science. According to Frederic Harrison, Lewes has shown that 'all Science is an ideal construction very far removed from a real transcript of facts'.[58] The 'ideal' nature of the scientific concept of the world is, rather impatiently, conceded by Huxley, talking about his difficulties of thought about 'materialism':

On the one hand, the notion of matter without force seemed to resolve the world into a set of geometrical ghosts, too dead even to jabber. On the other hand, Boscovich's hypothesis, by which matter was resolved into centres of force, was very attractive. But when one came to think it out, what in the world became of force considered as an objective entity? Force, even the most materialistic of philosophers will agree with the most idealistic, is nothing but a name for the cause of motion. And if, with Boscovich, I resolved things into centres of force, then matter vanished altogether and left immaterial entities in its place. One might as well frankly accept Idealism and have done with it.[59]

The role of 'idealism' in science is also stressed by Tyndall. In his 'Apology for the Belfast Address', he says he has been blamed for 'crossing the boundary of the experimental evidence' in the 'Address', and he answers the charge like this:

This, I reply, is the habitual action of the scientific mind ... in physics the experiential incessantly leads to the ultra-experiential; ... out of experience there always grows something finer than mere experience, and ... in their different powers of ideal extension consists, for the most part, the difference between the great and the mediocre investigator. The kingdom of science, then, cometh not by observation and experiment alone, but is completed by fixing the roots of observation and experiment in a region inaccessible to both, and in dealing with which we are forced to fall back upon the picturing power of the mind.[60]

This 'ultra-experiential' power of the scientific Imagination is also commented on by Frederick Pollock, in his Introduction to Clifford's *Lectures and Essays*:

Science and Poetry are own sisters; insomuch that in those branches of scientific enquiry which are the most abstract, most formal, and most remote from the grasp of the ordinary sensible imagination, a higher power of imagination, akin to the creative insight of the poet is most needed and most fruitful of lasting work. This living and constructive energy projects itself out into the world at the same time that it assimilates the surrounding world to itself.[61]

Here both creative energy and visionary insight are seen as attributes of the scientific Imagination. Tyndall links the two qualities in his lecture 'On the Scientific Use of the Imagination': 'We can magnify, diminish, qualify, and combine experiences, so as to render them fit for purposes entirely new. In explaining sensible phenomena, we habitually form images of the ultra sensible.'[62]

But how are these images to be formed, how are we to picture what is invisible and unknown? The obvious answer is by the use of analogy, of metaphors from what is known and seen. The scientist, like the poet, uses metaphors. In Tyndall's article on 'Matter and Force', he tries to imagine how these concepts originated in men's minds. When man first begins to ask questions about the causes of phenomena, Tyndall says, he finds 'that besides the phenomena which address the senses, there are laws and principles and processes which do not address the senses at all, but which must be, and can be, spiritually discerned'. Man tries to describe these processes by using analogies – for instance, by speaking of magnetic 'forces', taking an analogy from the forces of his own muscles, their power to 'push' or 'pull' as the magnet does, so that 'by a kind of poetic transfer, he applies to things external to himself, conceptions derived from himself'.[63] The analogies of science can also be drawn from the external world. In the lecture 'On the Scientific Use of the Imagination', Tyndall suggests that the 'wave-theory' of light is based on an analogy with the theory of sound as waves travelling through the air, which in turn is based on an analogy with visible ripples moving through water. Thus the invisible waves of sound moving through the invisible air, and the invisible waves of light moving through an invisible 'ether', can be imaginatively apprehended.[64] Similarly, Huxley sees a process of imaginative reconstruction through analogy working in geology and evolutionary biology. In his essay 'On the Method of Zadig', he speaks of 'all those sciences which have been termed historical or palaetiological, because they are retrospectively prophetic and strive towards the reconstruction in human imagination of events which have vanished and ceased to be', and he defends this use of the word 'prophecy' by defining it like this: 'the apprehension of that which lies out of the sphere of immediate knowledge; the seeing of that which, to the natural sense of the seer, is invisible.' Once again, science must go beyond the immediate evidence: and this method of retrospective prophecy 'is simple reasoning from analogy', from present conditions to those in the past.[65] A good example of the workings of the 'retrospectively prophetic' Imagination is Huxley's talk 'On a Piece of Chalk'. Here, he reasons from a known and familiar object, through comparisons with processes now going on, to the history of changes in the geographical and organic worlds. From the piece of chalk, he takes us to minute organisms now living in the depths of the Atlantic Ocean; reconstructs for us four vast alternations of sea and land; finds evidence of extinct species in the chalk; and leads us on to the theory of evolution, by analogy between changes in the in-organic and organic worlds. He concludes modestly:

A small beginning has led us to a great ending. If I were to put the bit of chalk with which we started into the hot but obscure flame of burning hydrogen, it would presently shine like the sun. It seems to me that this physical meta-morphosis is no false image of what has been the result of our subjecting it to a jet of fervent, though no-wise brilliant, thought to-night. It has become luminous, and its clear rays, penetrating the abyss of the remote past, have brought within our ken some stages of the evolution of the earth.[66]

The scientific Imagination can irradiate particular facts, and cast light on the remote past.

The lecture 'On a Piece of Chalk' exemplifies also Huxley's teaching technique. As he says in 'The Study of Zoology', 'The great matter is, to make teaching real and practical, by fixing the attention of the student on particular facts; but at the same time it should be rendered broad and comprehensive, by constant reference to the generalisations of which all particular facts are illustrations.'[67] This movement between particular fact and general theory, the visible and the invisible, the real and the ideal, characterises the scientific Imagaination. It is not 'unbridled' or 'arbitrary', since it must always grow from and refer back to particular objective facts. Victorian scientists tend not to commit themselves as to which comes first, fact or theory: they are interdependent, each growing from the other. Tyndall says that 'out of experience there always grows something finer than mere experience', but then goes on to fix 'the roots of observation and experiment in a region inaccessible to both', the region of imaginative vision.[68] The Imagination of the scientist, as well as being bound by reference to particular experimental facts, is also limited because its chief creation is the unifying concept of coherent, rational order. The 'ideal' world of scientific theory is constructed by Reason and Imagination working together. As Tyndall says, after explaining the theory of light, 'that composite and creative power, in which reason and imagination are united, has, we believe, led us into a world not less real than that of the senses'.[69] If the scientific Imagination is working within and helping to create a concept of universal, rational, harmonious order, it is not likely to dream up such fantastic violations of order as Frankenstein's monster. Monsters are more likely to be created by the purely subjective Imagination which does not bring its creations to the test of Nature's truth and law, imposing instead its own 'figments of superstitious dread', or dream palaces, onto Nature.

(vi) Contradictions and tensions

The scientific world view we have just been looking at is of its essence ordered, limited and coherent. Nevertheless, it contains within itself inevitable contradictions and tensions, which provide loop-holes for complexity, ambiguity and even 'super-naturalism' to creep back in. This is what makes it productive as a basis for works of art. An example of one of these 'tensions' is the opposition between the concept of 'fixed' law pervading the universe, most often imaged as a 'chain' of cause and effect, and the contrasting concept of universal 'organism', imaged as a 'tree', constantly growing and changing. The scientific writers seem to hold both these concepts in mind simultaneously – though there is also a sense in which they move from the first to the second, from a more reductive to a less reductive model. A circular process is going on: all the emotional and aesthetic considerations rejected in order to perceive the scientific world view are then rediscovered in a different guise within that world view. We can illustrate this thought process from Clifford's notebooks:

Every time that analysis strips from nature the gilding that we prized, she is forging thereout a new picture more glorious than before, to be suddenly revealed by the advent of a new sense whereby we see it – a new creation, at the sight of which the sons of God shall have cause to shout for joy.

What now shall I say of this new-grown perception of Law, which finds the infinite in a speck of dust, and the acts of eternity in every second of time?

He realises that this perception of Law at first seemingly 'kills our sense of the beautiful and takes all the romance out of nature'; but he asks whether the new perception may not eventually become

organic and unconscious, so that the sense of law becomes a direct perception? Shall we not then be really seeing something new? Shall there not be a new revelation of a greater and more perfect cosmos, a universe freshborn, a new heaven and a new earth? *Mors janua vitae*; by death to this world we enter upon a new life in the next.[70]

Clifford is talking about a 'new' vision, but only the old religious terminology is adequate to describe it. His progression from 'stripping off' of religious 'gilding', through a depressing, reductive naturalism, to a rediscovery of the lost 'supernatural' values in the new naturalistic world view, is of course reminiscent of Carlyle. In *Sartor Resartus*, Teufelsdröckh similarly advocates the removal of outworn religious 'clothing', and passes through a time of despair to a new vision of 'Natural Supernaturalism'.[71] This process of rediscovery seems to be central to the construction of the Victorian scientific world view. Huxley, in a letter to Kingsley, tells how '*Sartor Resartus* led me to know that a deep sense of religion was compatible with the entire absence of theology.'[72] As we have seen, Huxley's chief aim was 'the resolute facing of the world as it is when the garment of make-believe by which pious hands have hidden its uglier features is stripped off'.[73] But when he wants to describe the new vision of science he reverts to the language of 'make-believe': he calls science a 'Cinderella', and Theology and Philosophy take the roles of the ugly sisters:

in her garret, she has fairy visions out of the ken of the pair of shrews who are quarrelling downstairs. She sees the order which pervades the seeming disorder of the world; the great drama of evolution, with its full share of pity and terror, but also with abundant goodness and beauty, unrolls itself before her eyes.[74]

Of course, Huxley is being fanciful and metaphorical here – but I think that the metaphorical use of 'supernatural' language by scientific writers does express a real sense of wonder and mystery that takes us beyond reductionism. Certainly in the passage from Clifford's notebooks the merely natural is seen as transfigured into something utterly 'new'. The essential strangeness and mysteriousness of what is revealed by scientific explanation is insisted on by Tyndall. In his 'Recollections of Carlyle', he speaks of Carlyle's fear that science tended to destroy ' "transcendent wonder" '. Tyndall would counter this by pointing out that 'preoccupation alone could close the eyes of the student of natural science to the fact that the long line of his researches is, in reality, a line of wonders'.[75] In his article on 'Matter and Force', Tyndall again stresses that 'It is the function of science, not as some think to divest this universe of its wonder and mystery, but ... to point out the wonder and mystery of common things.'[76] In an almost Wordsworthian manner, the scientist finds in the merely commonplace and natural a gateway to the transcendental and mysterious.

But as well as finding mystery within the scientific framework, the scientific writers admitted that mystery lay outside their framework, beyond the limits they had chosen to draw. They did not see science as an inclusive account of all experience and existence – beyond scientific explanation was what Herbert Spencer called 'The Unknowable'.[77] This is how Tyndall puts it:

As regards knowledge, physical science is polar. In one sense it knows, or is destined to know, everything. In another sense it knows nothing. Science understands much of this intermediate phase of things that we call nature, of which it is the product; but science knows nothing of the origin or destiny of nature. Who or what made the sun and gave his rays their alleged power? Who or what made and bestowed upon the ultimate particles of matter their wondrous power of varied interaction? Science does not know: the mystery, though pushed back, remains unaltered.[78]

To express our sense of this mystery, Tyndall allows the symbolic use of religious conceptions:

And if ... the human mind, with the yearning of a pilgrim for his distant home, will still turn to the Mystery from which it has emerged, seeking so to fashion it as to give unity to thought and faith; so long as this is done ... with the enlightened recognition that ultimate fixity of conception is here un-attainable, and that each succeeding age must be held free to fashion the mystery in accordance with its own needs – then, casting aside the restrictions of Materialism, I would affirm this to be a field for the noblest exercise of what, in contrast with the *knowing* faculties, may be called the *creative* faculties of man.[79]

Edward Dowden shows a similar attitude: he is considering 'the modification by science of our conception, not of the world only, nor of man, but of the Supreme Power':

Recognising all our notions of this inscrutable Power as but symbolic, we may for purposes of edification accept an anthropomorphic conception, and yield to all that, in sincerity, and imposing no delusion upon ourselves, such an anthropomorphic conception may suggest ... . Nor will it be without an enlarging and liberating power with our spirit from time to time ... if we part with, dismiss or abolish the symbolic conception suggested by man, in favour of one which the life and beauty of this earth of ours, or of the sublime cosmos of which it is a member, may suggest to the devout imagination.[80]

The 'Supreme Power' is one of the 'mysteries' science cannot explain; another is human consciousness. Huxley points this out when he defends himself against a charge of rejecting 'everything beyond the bounds of physical science':

Nobody, I imagine, will credit me with a desire to limit the empire of physical science, but I really feel bound to confess that a great many very familiar and, at the same time, extremely important phenomena lie quite beyond its legitimate limits. I cannot conceive, for example, how the pheno-mena of consciousness, as such and apart from the physical process by which they are called into existence, are to be brought within the bounds of physical science.

As an example of such inexplicable phenomena Huxley cites the feeling of beauty:

I do not suppose that I am exceptionally endowed because I have all my life enjoyed a keen perception of the beauty offered us by nature and by art. Now physical science may and probably will, some day, enable our posterity to set forth the exact physical concomitants and conditions of the strange rapture of beauty. But if ever that day arrives, the rapture will remain, just as it is now, outside and beyond the physical world; and, even in the mental world, something superadded to mere sensation.[81]

So mental and physical events must be seen, as Huxley puts it elsewhere, to 'run, not in one series, but along two parallel lines', between which is an inexplicable bridge.[82] Tyndall makes the same point in his 'Belfast Address': 'You cannot satisfy the human understanding in its demand for logical continuity between molecular processes and the phenomena of consciousness. This is a rock on which Materialism must inevitably split.'[83] And Clifford also attacks 'that singular Materialism of high authority and recent date which makes consciousness a physical agent, "correlates" it with Light and Nerve-force, and so reduces it to an objective phenomenon'.[84] Here again Tyndall sees room for the symbolic reintroduction of religious language. He considers the mysterious interaction of mental and physical phenomena, and remarks:

Observation proves that they interact, but in passing from one to the other, we meet a blank which mechanical deduction is unable to fill. Frankly stated, we have here to deal with facts almost as difficult to be seized mentally as the idea of a soul, and if you are content to make your 'soul' a poetic rendering of a phenomenon which refuses the yoke of ordinary physical laws, I, for one, would not object to this exercise of ideality ... .

Though misuse may render it grotesque or insincere, the idealisation of ancient conceptions, when done consciously and above board, has, in my opinion, an important future.[85]

Tyndall has a similar tolerance for whole mythologies – of the Greek mythology he says: 'As poets, the priesthood would have been justified, their deities, celestial and otherwise, with all their retinue and appliances, being more or less legitimate symbols and personifications of the aspects of nature and the phases of the human soul.'[86]

Huxley is just as tolerant of religious terminology if used symbolically, and his recognition that ultimately scientific terminology is *also* symbolic helps to justify this tolerance:

I suppose that, so long as the human mind exists, it will not escape its deep-seated instinct to personify its intellectual conceptions. The science of the present day is as full of this particular form of intellectual shadow-worship as is the nescience of ignorant ages. The difference is that the philosopher who is worthy of the name knows that his personified hypotheses, such as law, and force, and ether, and the like, are merely useful symbols, while the ignorant and the careless take them for adequate expressions of reality. So, it may be, that the majority of mankind may find the practice of morality made easier by the use of theological symbols. And unless these are converted from symbols into idols, I do not see that science has anything to say to the practice, except to give an occasional warning of its dangers.[87]

Here subjectivity disturbs the coherence of the scientific world picture in another way – scientific concepts are seen to be symbols created by the human mind. As we saw, the very concept of a coherent natural order is a construct of the scientific Imagination. The scientist sees what he has chosen to see: his choice to see 'objective' facts and rational law is based on his belief in their value. The scientific world view is both solidly based on Nature's truth and law; and precariously based on human choice, a conscious limitation to certain ways of seeing Nature. This implies that other ways of seeing, other choices of symbols, might be equally valid. Here the scientists would reply that their way of seeing is preferable because of its *results* – as Huxley says:

If we find that the ascertainment of the order of nature is facilitated by using one terminology, or one set of symbols, rather than another, it is our clear duty to use the former, and no harm can accrue, so long as we bear in mind, that we are dealing merely with terms and symbols.[88]

But this still begs the question, why choose the 'ascertainment of the order of nature' as a goal? In the end, the choice of 'symbols' is a matter of intuition, as even Huxley can admit when he compares moral and physical law in rather a surprising way:

morality is based on feeling, not on reason; though reason alone is competent to trace out the effects of our actions and thereby dictate conduct. Justice is founded on the love of one's neighbour; and goodness is a kind of beauty. The moral law, *like the laws of physical nature*, rests in the long run upon instinctive intuitions, and is neither more nor less 'innate' and 'necessary' than they are.[89]

The scientific world picture is ultimately based on a subjective belief in the values of objectivity, rationality and order. By staying within certain limits, these values can be preserved. As Tyndall says:

The mind of man may be compared to a musical instrument with a certain range of notes, beyond which in both directions we have an infinitude of silence. The phenomena of matter and force lie within our intellectual range ... . But behind, and above, and around all, the real mystery of the universe lies unsolved, and as far as we are concerned, is incapable of solution.[90]

The scientists choose to stay within this musical range in order to achieve harmony. But the possibility of other choices involving disharmony and mystery remains as a necessary background to their world picture.

And even within their picture all is not as coherent as at first appears. Once again, it is the existence of human consciousness that disturbs the pattern. As we have seen, man was felt to be linked to Nature by a fundamental kinship: materially, he was of the same composition as the rest of Nature, and organically he was part of the family of living species. In order not to admit any 'supernatural' breaks in the continuity of evolution, man's mental and moral qualities had similarly to be derived from a 'natural' basis. So Darwin, in *The Descent of Man*, derives moral behaviour from the evolution of the social instincts;[91] and in *The Expression of the Emotions*, he collects evidence of moral behaviour in animals in order to establish a continuum leading up to man.[92] As Edward Clodd puts it, 'the links in the chain of psychical life between man and the creatures beneath him are unbroken'.[93] Mind, like body, has been evolved through a process of adaptation to the environment. This belief is central to Herbert Spencer's system of psychology: 'the human brain is an organised register of infinitely-numerous experiences received during the evolution of that series of organisms through which the human organism has been reached.' This gives the mind certain 'pre-established relations' with the external world.[94] Mind, like body, is inseparably part of Nature, evolved from and adapted to the outside world. Yet, as J.D.Y. Peel points out in his book, *Herbert Spencer – The Evolution of a Sociologist*,

When we compare Spencer's *Psychology* with any modern textbook on the subject, we are at once struck by the absolutely dominating place in it that is occupied by the explanation of the conscious operations of thought. Yet this is set within a naturalistic framework of explanation which presents thinking as being only different in degree from feeling, and as a response to the environment which should be compared with those of the lowest animals and the humblest plants.[95]

Thus, on the one hand, the scientific writers see the mind as an organic product of Nature, working by instinct; on the other, they praise the conscious, rational, objective thinking of the scientific mind which constructs theories *about* Nature. There seem to be two quite different ways in which the human mind relates to Nature which need not necessarily be in harmony.

This uncomfortable split is in fact inherent in the attempt to apply evolutionary theory to human mental and moral development. Consciousness introduces a new factor and a new kind of process. In *The Descent of Man*, Darwin agrees with Wallace

that man after he had partially acquired those intellectual and moral faculties which distinguish him from the lower animals, would have been but little liable to bodily modifications through natural selection or any other means. For man is enabled through his mental faculties 'to keep with an unchanged body in harmony with the changing universe'.[96]

And Darwin recognises that the intellectual and moral faculties change by a different kind of process:

Important as the struggle for existence has been and even still is, yet as far as the highest part of man's nature is concerned there are other agencies more important. For the moral qualities are advanced, either directly or indirectly, much more through the effects of habit, the reasoning powers, instruction, religion, etc., than through natural selection.[97]

Huxley, in the 'Prolegomena' to his lecture on 'Evolution and

Ethics', also makes a distinction between the struggle for existence, which he calls 'the cosmic process', and 'the ethical process' in society. The ethical process, as opposed to the cosmic 'survival of the fittest', is directed 'to the fitting of as many as possible to survive'.[98] Conscious moral intention works against the 'natural' direction of evolution. Of course, Huxley would probably still claim that there is an underlying order connecting both processes; and even if the process of natural selection is not relevant to human moral development, this does not invalidate what Huxley says elsewhere of the moral relevance of scientific thought. Paradoxically, scientific thought itself is one of those intellectual, conscious processes that have detached themselves from the natural process which is itself the object and creation of scientific thought. Again, there is a sense of a curious gap, which perhaps could be filled by a theory of the unconscious. As Huxley says, mental and physical events 'run, not in one series, but along two parallel lines',[99] and evolutionary theory seems unable to provide a bridge. Our two different, parallel bonds to Nature, by physical origin and by scientific understanding, remain a source of tension and complexity.

CHAPTER 2

Tennyson

On Tennyson's death in 1892, Huxley summed up his enthusiastic admiration for Tennyson's poetry like this: 'He was the only modern poet, in fact I think the only poet since the time of Lucretius, who has taken the trouble to understand the work and tendency of the men of science.'[1] In a letter to Hallam Tennyson, Tyndall was equally enthusiastic about Tennyson's scientific accuracy in observation: 'In regard to metaphors drawn from science, your father, like Carlyle, made sure of their truth. To secure accuracy, he spared no pains.'[2] We have seen that Dowden finds evidence in Tennyson's poetry of the influence of 'The Scientific Movement', in Tennyson's imaginative response to leading concepts of the Victorian scientific world view, such as gradualism and natural law.[3] Prominent Victorian agnostics saw *In Memoraim* as expressing their own cast of mind, giving voice to their hopes and fears.[4] It is this Tennyson that I hope to recreate in this chapter, Tennyson as Huxley and Tyndall must have read him, an agnostic, scientific Tennyson, who shared their world view, and explored more fully its emotional and spiritual dimensions.

Of course, it is true that Tennyson also had many reservations about the tendencies of contemporary science. As Tyndall wrote to Hallam Tennyson, 'Your father's interest in science was profound, but not, I believe, unmingled with fear of its "materialistic" tendencies.'[5] But this aspect of Tennyson's response to science has been overstressed, and some of the evidence for it misinterpreted. For instance, this quotation from Hallam Tennyson's *Memoir* is used to illustrate Tennyson's alleged repudiation of Darwin's 'materialistic' theory:[6] 'To Tyndall he once said, "No evolutionist is able to explain the mind of Man or how any possible physiological change of tissue can produce conscious thought." '[7] When this is quoted out of context it also sounds as if Tennyson is attacking Tyndall as a representative of scientific materialism, and flooring him with a clever argument. However, as we have seen, what Tennyson is saying here is a point repeatedly made by Tyndall himself – and one that did not prevent Tyndall from accepting Darwinism. The correspondence of thought between Tennyson and Tyndall is in fact made quite clear in the *Memoir* in a footnote: Hallam Tennyson quotes from Tyndall's *Scientific Materialism*:

But the passage from the physics of the brain to the corresponding facts of consciousness is unthinkable, granted that a definite thought and a definite molecular action in the brain occur simultaneously; we do not possess the intellectual organ, nor apparently any rudiment of the organ, which would enable us to pass, by a process of reasoning, from the one to the other. They appear together, but we do not know why.[8]

　　Far from attacking Tyndall, Tennyson's remark is either echoing something Tyndall has already said to him, or asking for reassurance and confirmation from Tyndall. The two men were friends, so it is most unlikely Tennyson was unaware of Tyndall's almost identical viewpoint. Hallam Tennyson records a charming example of their conversation, ranging over all subjects, spiritual, metaphysical and scientific:

To-day Tyndall said to him, 'God and spirit I know, and matter I know; and I believe in both.' And in answer to my father's profession of belief in 'individual immortality' Tyndall remarked, 'We may all be absorbed into the Godhead.' My father said, 'Suppose that He is the real person, and we are only relatively personal.' He talked with Tyndall then about experiments as to the origin of life – having frequently inspected Tyndall's hermetically-sealed bottles: and it interested him that Tyndall was convinced that life could not originate without life.[9]

The scientist's interest in the details of metaphysical speculations about the spiritual realm, and the poet's interest in the physical details of scientific experiment, are particularly surprising and illuminating here, as is the easy and natural transition of the conversation from one realm to another, from spiritual to scientific.

This is presumably the kind of discussion which took place at the Metaphysical Society, founded in 1869, of which Tennyson, Tyndall, Huxley, Clifford, John Morley and Leslie Stephen were all members. Tennyson's poem 'De Profundis' may have been influenced by his membership of the Society;[10] in any case, this poem, begun in 1852 but not published until 1880, seems to me to give form to the metaphysical problems touched upon in Tennyson's informal discussions with Tyndall, and thus to symbolise in its two-part structure one of the major areas of tension within the Victorian scientific world view. Like Tennyson's remark to Tyndall it can be misread as an illustration of Tennyson's rejection of science.

The poem is addressed to Tennyson's newly-born son, and takes the form of 'Two Greetings', a 'materialistic' one, and a parallel but separate 'spiritual' one. Here is the first:

I

Out of the deep, my child, out of the deep,
Where all that was to be, in all that was,
Whirl'd for a million aeons thro' the vast
Waste dawn of multitudinous-eddying light
Out of the deep, my child, out of the deep,
Thro' all this changing world of changeless law,
And every phase of ever-heightening life,
And nine long months of antenatal gloom,
With this last moon, this crescent – her dark orb
Touch'd with earth's light – thou comest, darling boy;
. . . and may
The fated channel where thy motion lives
Be prosperously shaped, and sway thy course
Along the years of haste and random youth,
Unshatter'd; then full-current through full man;
And last in kindly curves, with gentlest fall,

> By quiet fields, a slowly-dying power,
> To that last deep where we and thou are still.

The material universe is not seen here as depressing, restricting or irrelevant to human growth. On the contrary, it is beautiful, mutable but ordered, and potentially vital. The evolutionary processes, beginning with the evolution of the cosmos, moving on through organic evolution, now recapitulated by the ante-natal development of the foetus, flower finally into a human life. As in the scientific writings, man is seen as essentially akin to Nature, developing from it and determined by it. This vision of organic, evolutionary unity is very similar to the scientific world view – as Tyndall puts it, 'all our philosophy, all our poetry, all our science, all our art – Plato, Shakespeare, Newton and Raphael – are potential in the fires of the sun'; and 'life and thought' are 'the very flower' of 'matter and force', since 'the animal world is, so to say, a distillation through the vegetable world from inorganic nature'.[11] Moreover, Tennyson's Universe, like Tyndall's, is structured by 'changeless law' in the midst of incessant change, 'the law which reveals immutability in the midst of change', as Tyndall says of the conservation of energy.[12] In 'De Profundis', man's life is seen as determined by Nature, limited by a 'fated channel'; but human life has its own 'motion' and 'power' that co-operates in the course laid out for it. Life is seen as a physical force, perhaps an energy-wave, playing its part in the living Universe of matter and force.

As in the scientific writings, this Universe of living matter, including man, appears at first to be totally coherent and unified, but then reveals another, contradictory, dimension. Tennyson introduces this other dimenstion in the second part of his poem, his second 'Greeting':

II

i

> Out of the deep, my child, out of the deep,
> From that great deep, before our world begins,
> Whereon the Spirit of God moves as he will –
> Out of the deep, my child, out of the deep,

From that true world within the world we see,
Whereof our world is but the bounding shore –
Out of the deep, Spirit, out of the deep,
With this ninth moon, that sends the hidden sun
Down yon dark sea, thou comest, darling boy.

ii

For in the world, which is not ours, They said
'Let us make man' and that which should be man,
From that one light no man can look upon,
Drew to this shore lit by the suns and moons
And all the shadows. O dear Spirit half-lost
In thine own shadow and this fleshly sign
That thou art thou – who wailest being born
And banish'd into mystery, and the pain
Of this divisible-indivisible world
Among the numerable-innumerable
Sun, sun, and sun, thro' finite-infinite space
In finite-infinite Time – our mortal veil
And shatter'd phantom of that infinite One,
Who made thee inconceivably thyself
Out of his whole World-self and all in all –
Live thou! and of the grain and husk, the grape
And ivyberry, choose; and still depart
From death to death thro' life and life, and find
Nearer and every nearer Him, who wrought
Not Matter, nor the finite-infinite,
But this main-miracle, that thou art thou,
With power on thine own act and on the world.

On a superficial reading we could assume that what Tennyson is doing here is repudiating the scientific, materialistic, naturalistic world view, by adding onto it this extra supernatural dimension of his own. But what is more striking to me is the way his approach corresponds to that of the scientific writers. The 'supernatural' is not allowed in any way to *intervene* in the material continuum of the first part, but instead remains totally separate and yet parallel to that material universe. Tennyson introduces this supernatural dimension in order to account for ultimate causation, and for individual consciousness – 'that thou art thou' – with its power of free will 'on thine own act and on the world'. As we saw, these are precisely the areas of 'The Unknowable' which the scientific writers admit they cannot explain. Beyond the limits of their coherent world picture, lies ultimate mystery, as Tyndall says:

As regards knowledge, physical science is polar. In one sense it knows, or is destined to know, everything. In another sense it knows nothing. Science understands much of this intermediate phase of things that we call nature, of which it is the product; but science knows nothing of the origin or destiny of nature. Who or what made the sun and gave his rays their alleged power? Who or what made and bestowed upon the ultimate particles of matter their wondrous power of varied interaction? Science does not know: the mystery, though pushed back, remains unaltered.[13]

The first part of Tennyson's poem describes the 'intermediate phase of things that we call nature'; the second part is an attempt to formulate answers to some of these ultimate questions that Tyndall asks. In doing so, Tennyson is only taking on the role that Tyndall allows to the poet:

And if ... the human mind, with the yearning of a pilgrim for his distant home, will still turn to the Mystery from which it has emerged, seeking so to fashion it as to give unity to thought and faith; so long as this is done ... with the enlightened recognition that ultimate fixity of conception is here unattainable, and that each succeeding age must be held free to fashion the mystery in accordance with its own needs – then, casting aside the restrictions of Materialism, I would affirm this to be a field for a noblest exercise of what, in contrast with the *knowing* faculties, may be called the *creative* faculties of man.[14]

Tennyson's images of 'the deep', 'the world, which is not ours', 'They', 'that infinite One', 'His whole World-self', are his creative attempt 'to fashion the mystery', while the agnostic vagueness of his formulations ensures that there is no prescriptive 'fixity' about his conceptions.

The individual consciousness, as well as the ultimate cause, was admitted to be an inexplicable mystery by the scientific writers. Huxley is unable to conceive 'how the phenomena of consciousness, as such and apart from the physical process by which they are called into existence, are to be brought within the bounds of physical science'. In his view, mental and physical events 'run, not in one series, but along two parallel lines'.[15] This image of parallelism neatly describes the structure of Tennyson's 'De Profundis'. Parallelism seems to have been one way the scientific writers resolved the awkward tension between the explicable and the inexplicable, the physical and the mental, in their world view. By keeping the two parts of his poem separate, complete in themselves yet parallel, Tennyson shows his sympathy with that world view. As we have seen, parallelism emerges as a theme in his informal conversations with Tyndall – 'God and spirit' parallel to 'matter', 'conscious thought' parallel to 'physiological change'. In both cases, the two sides of the parallel are both allowed an equal reality, but are separated by an inexplicable, unbridgeable gap, like the two parallel 'Greetings' of 'De Profundis'.

'De Profundis', as I have said, belong to roughly the same period as the scientific writings I have described in chapter 1, and also to the period of Tennyson's friendship with Tyndall and Huxley. But many of the poems of Tennyson which show the most close and interesting interconnections with science belong to an earlier period. As has often been pointed out, Tennyson's most famous references to science are pre-Darwinian; and the scientific writings which can be shown to have influenced his poetry most were written by an earlier set of writers[16] than the group centred on Huxley and Tyndall. These early Victorian scientific writers, apart from Lyell, were writing within the tradition of Natural Theology – they offered the facts and ideas of science not as the basis for a new, autonomous world view, but as evidence in support of an existing world view, as proofs of God's benevolent design. Thus it is possible to argue that Tennyson's positive response to science is to this earlier, teleological, theological science; while his negative response is reserved for the newer, agnostic naturalistic science emerging in the work of Lyell, and culminating in Darwin and his popularisers.[17]

But this is to assume that the earlier science writers themselves showed no trace of the new scientific world view. While they were carrying on the tradition of Paley (whose *Natural Theology* appeared in 1802), new discoveries and new ideas in science made their approach and emphasis very different from him. This significant difference has been pointed out by Susan Gliserman in her analysis of the writings of Roget and Whewell, two early Victorian science writers whose influence is clear in *In Memoriam*. She sees Paley's approach as having been essentially 'mechanistic', bringing up 'examples of useful structures haphazardly', in his attempt to portray God as the Craftsman of the Universe. Paley lacks any conception of organic unity in Nature:

The major shift from Paley to Roget is from a mechanistic metaphor to a vital one. For Roget 'living Nature' is 'everywhere characterised by boundless variety, by inscrutable complexity, by perpetual mutation'.... By being fully open to all the scientific evidence, he must revise the 'great chain of being' as a metaphor in zoology, and in doing so brings it closer to a Darwinian conception of branching development.[18]

Similarly, Whewell is

clearly aware of the coherence of the scientific perspective. Whewell's universe in its complex interaction of laws and in the excitement and wonder it generates is much closer to Roget's than to Paley's idea of a world of simple mechanical contrivances.

Whewell's work is informed by 'an idea of an organic unified cosmos which exists for itself as well as to create a positive environment for man. The autonomy of the universe is apparent in Whewell's explanations of the complexity of its system of laws.'[19] This potentially autonomous universe, with its organic unity, changeability, and complex coherence is remarkably similar to the 'naturalistic' universe of Tyndall and Huxley. In fact, Gliserman goes on to suggest that the theological aims of Roget and Whewell were in danger of subversion by the new scientific universe they were presenting.

So Tennyson, in assimilating the prevailing scientific world view through these and other writers, was in some ways moving towards the same vision as that reached by Tyndall and Huxley – like Carlyle, he may even have helped to form it. It is interesting to reflect that while Darwin was brooding over his theory of evolution from 1839 to 1859, as he worked towards *The Origin of Species*, from 1833 to 1850 Tennyson was also brooding over problems of geology and evolution as he composed *In Memoriam*. Both men were well-versed in both Paley and Lyell, and had read the evolutionary speculations of Chambers; and both works are in a sense the product of the same background, the same ways of thinking and seeing. Thus Tennyson was not influenced or converted by Tyndall and Huxley; instead, he had already adopted various aspects of their world view, and was hailed by them as a kindred spirit.

In Memoriam is certainly a 'gradualist' poem in its vision of Nature and in its structure. As Culler says, '*In Memoriam* is to *Lycidas* as Lyell's *Principles of Geology* is to the Mosaic cosmogony. It operates not by means of volcanic eruptions and deluges but by subsidence and erosion.'[20] Hence the vast length of the poem, as compared to earlier elegies such as *Lycidas*. The elegaic transition from grief to reconciliation cannot be accomplished suddenly; instead, it is built up slowly and almost indiscernably through the 131 stanzas, until by the end we find that the many small units have accumulated and interacted to produce a new whole, a new mood of acceptance and integration. The images of geological gradualism that Culler uses to describe this structure – 'subsidence and erosion' – are in no way arbitrary, for Tennyson uses such imagery himself within the poem. It is not just that Tennyson uses metaphors from Nature to describe his state of mind, but that throughout the poem Tennyson's thoughts and feelings about the death of his friend Hallam are parallelled by an exploration of his thoughts and feelings regarding the scientific world picture as presented by Lyell and other writers. And, just as his feelings about Hallam's death change gradually from grief to reconciliation, so his feelings about the scientific universe change from fear and depression to acceptance and celebration. As with the later scientific writers, this acceptance involves the perception of ordered law, patterned interconnection, and organic process, giving structure and stability to the changes of a mutable and transient universe.

The parallelism between the descriptions of Nature's processes and the descriptions of Tennyson's states of mind suggest that the former could be read as a continued metaphor for the latter. But it is also possible to reverse this reading and see Tennyson as gradually adjusting his thought-processes into harmony with Nature, so that his inner life becomes an analogy or 'type' of the ordered processes of the natural world. As Tyndall puts it, 'The world was built in order: and to us are trusted the will and the power to discern its harmonies, and to make them the lessons of our lives.'[21] But, as we have seen, 'the power to discern its harmonies' is only given to those who have to some extent *already* adjusted their perceptions into harmony with Nature. To those without an objective, organic vision, the universe of science will appear harsh and disordered, unable to fulfil their supernatural expectations and 'preconceived notions'. This further complication is also present in *In Memoriam*: it is Tennyson's subjective state of grief and shock at the beginning of the poem that causes him to see Nature as hostile and chaotic. As he comes to accept Hallam's death, and takes a larger perspective on human life, so he comes to perceive a larger order in Nature. The realisation that human life must go on is parallelled by his celebration of process and evolution in Nature. By contrast, in his initial state of shock he longed for fixity, and thus saw Nature as a destructive, unstable power.

This longing for fixity is evident in the very first stanza:

> I held it truth, with him who sings
>   To one clear harp in divers tones,
>   That men may rise on stepping stones
> Of their dead selves to higher things.
>
> But who shall so forecast the years
>   And find in loss a gain to match?
>   Or reach a hand thro' time to catch
> The far-off interest of tears?
>
> Let Love clasp Grief lest both be drown'd,
>   Let darkness keep her raven gloss:

Ah, sweeter to be drunk with loss,
To dance with death, to beat the ground,

Than that the victor Hours should scorn
The long result of love, and boast,
'Behold the man that loved and lost,
But all he was is overworn.'

Tennyson begins by telling us of his previous faith in gradualism, in lines from which Dowden quotes to elaborate his description of the 'scientific idea' of anti-revolutionary progress in Tennyson's poetry: 'No true reformation was ever sudden; let us innovate like nature and like time. Men may rise to higher things, not on wings, but on "Stepping-stones of their dead selves".'[22] At the beginning of *In Memoriam*, Tennyson finds little comfort in this gradualist faith: the end result of the long process is too 'far-off' to be of any conceivable help at present. Tennyson is often preoccupied with the problem of the tension between one's ability to imagine the future result of a gradual process and the necessity to reconcile oneself to small steps and incompletion in the present. This tension can produce overhasty impatience as one rushes towards the envisioned end, and tries unsuccessfully to reach it without going through the necessary slow process first. This seems to be the mistake of Princess Ida in *The Princess*. Or, as in stanza I of *In Memoriam*, the ability to 'forecast' or even desire the end result can be lost, in the overwhelming sense of the present. Of course, in both these cases, Tennyson is using gradualism as a model for a desirable, productive process, one that leads eventually to 'gain' and 'interest', out of the 'loss' and 'tears' of the intermediate stages. While his confidence in this sort of process has been shaken at the beginning of *In memoriam*, he retains a deep fear of purely negative, destructive gradual processes: eventually 'the victor Hours' will be able to

boast,
'Behold the man that loved and lost,
But all he was is overworn.'

Like a geological process of erosion, time will eventually wear away and obliterate Tennyson's love. This fear of gradual erosion and obliteration will be echoed in the way Tennyson describes Nature – he has lost his ability to see the gradual processes that are building up the new, and can only see the wearing away of the old. Productive processes are relegated to the past – his feeling for Hallam was 'the long result of love', the outcome of a gradual cumulative process. At this stage, Tennyson seems to see the world as consisting of gradual creative processes (love) whose results are then destroyed by gradual erosion (forgetfulness). He cannot see that the two processes may be simultaneous and interdependent.

In other ways, too, his perception of Nature's processes has been affected by his emotional state, as we find in stanza III:

> O sorrow, cruel fellowship,
>> O Priestess in the vaults of Death,
>> O sweet and bitter in a breath,
> What whispers from thy lying lip?
>
> 'The stars,' she whispers, 'blindly run;
>> A web is wov'n across the sky;
>> From out waste places comes a cry,
> And murmurs from the dying sun;
>
> 'And all the phantom, Nature, stands –
>> With all the music in her tone,
>> A hollow echo of my own, –
> A hollow form with empty hands.'

Here Tennyson presents us with a vision of a dead, mechanistic Universe. The constricting chains of law that regulate the movements of the stars are here 'wov'n' together to form a restrictive 'web'. The image of the web has none of the organic implications that George Eliot gives it, when she uses it as an image of society as a living tissue of which we each form a part.[23] Here it is an alien structure, separate from man, imprisoning him in a material world and perhaps also cutting him off from any larger source of meaning. But we must not forget that this image comes from the 'lying lips' of Tennyson's 'Sorrow'. As we saw in the first verse, his grief makes him want to stop participating in Nature's processes, to separate himself off in an unnatural fixity. Thus it is not surprising that Nature now appears separate and alien from him. The stars run blindly like the parts in a machine instead of performing a cosmic dance; the web of causation restricts and blinds man instead of connecting him with the living whole; Nature's processes are only destructive, as the 'waste places' and the 'dying sun' testify. The 'perception of Law' only 'kills our sense of the beautiful and takes all the romance out of nature',[24] as Clifford puts it; and, like Clifford, Tennyson is going to discover more positive ways of perceiving Law, as he learns to co-operate with the cosmic processes and harmonise his life with Nature's harmonies. But, at this stage, these harmonies seem to be only his own projections – Nature is only a metaphor for his moods, with no independent 'music': 'all the music in her tone, A hollow echo of my own'.

Tennyson is frightened by the idea of Nature as a destructive mechanism; he is also frightened by the idea of Nature as a random chaos, in stanzas XXXIV and L. He has dark visions in which

> 'earth is darkness at the core,
> And dust and ashes all that is;
>
> This round of green, this orb of flame,
> Fantastic beauty; such as lurks
> In some wild Poet when he works
> Without a conscience or an aim.'

Or he sees 'Time, a maniac scattering dust, And life a Fury slinging flame.' While not directly attributed to the voice of 'Sorrow', these visions too have subjective causes – the first is the result of a loss of belief in immortality; the second is produced by 'pangs that conquer trust'. And they also mirror Tennyson's own chaotic and confused emotional state, as he has described it in stanza XVI, when wonders whether the shock of his grief has

> made me that delirious man
> Whose fancy fuses old and new,

> And flashes into false and true,
> And mingles all without a plan?

The disordered universe that Tennyson fears also 'mingles all without a plan'; and he himself appears here as the 'wild Poet', 'without a conscience or an aim', that is his image for the universe in stanza xxxiv. This internal and external chaos will have resolved itself into dependable order by the end of the poem: like Huxley's personified 'Science', Tennyson will have a vision of 'the order which pervades the seeming disorder of the world'.[25]

But first all Tennyson's doubts and fears about Nature come to a head in stanzas LV and LVI:

> The wish that of the living whole
>   No life may fail beyond the grave,
>   Derives it not from what we have
> The likest God within the soul?
>
> Are God and Nature then at strife,
>   That Nature lends such evil dreams?
>   So careful of the type she seems,
> So careless of the single life;
>
> That I considering everywhere
>   Her secret meaning in her deeds,
>   And finding that of fifty seeds
> She often brings but one to bear,
>
> I falter where I firmly trod,
>   And falling with my weight of cares
>   Upon the great world's altar-stairs
> That slope through darkness up to God,
>
> I stretch lame hands of faith, and grope,
>   And gather dust and chaff, and call
>   To what I feel is Lord of all,
> And faintly trust the larger hope.
>
>   LVI
> 'So careful of the type'? but no,
>   From scarped cliff and quarried stone
>   She cries, 'A thousand types are gone:
> I care for nothing, all shall go.

'Thou makest thine appeal to me:
   I bring to life, I bring to death:
   The spirit does but mean the breath:
I know no more.' And he, shall he,

Man, her last work, who seem'd so fair,
   Such splendid purpose in his eyes,
   Who roll'd the psalm to wintry skies,
Who built him fanes of fruitless prayer,

Who trusted God was love indeed
   And love Creation's final law –
   Tho' Nature, red in tooth and claw
With ravine, shriek'd against his creed –

Who loved, who suffer'd countless ills,
   Who battled for the True, the Just,
   Be blown about the desert dust,
Or seal'd within the iron hills?

No more? A monster then, a dream,
   A discord. Dragons of the prime,
   That tare each other in their slime,
Were mellow music matched with him.

The images of Nature as a meaningless chaos, and Nature as a destructive mechanism, merge together here. Nature is seen as wasteful and 'careless', in her treatment of individuals: she is the scene of disorder and destruction. Man is not part of her harmony, he is a 'discord' amid the general pattern of destruction. Tennyson focuses especially on the destructive gradual process of extinction as recorded by the fossils in the rocks: 'A thousand types are gone.' Nature's message is only destruction, and a reductive materialism: 'The spirit does but mean the breath.' But this reductive picture is partly the result of Tennyson's asking the wrong questions: he is coming to Nature with supernatural expectations, looking for natural evidence of God's love and of man's immortality, in the manner of Natural Theology. Nature's remark, 'Thou makest thine appeal to me', implies Tennyson is asking the wrong question in the wrong place. And his description of himself 'considering everywhere Her secret meaning in her deeds' suggests that he may be supplying the sinister meanings he finds in Nature, from the frustration of his own emotional need for supernatural reassurance. By the end of the poem, Tennyson has explicitly repudiated Natural Theology as a way of finding God and of relating man to Nature:

CXXIV

I found him not in world or sun,
 Or eagle's wing, or insect's eye;
 Not thro' the questions men may try,
The petty cobwebs we have spun;

If e'er when faith had fall'n asleep,
 I heard a voice 'believe no more'
 And heard an ever-breaking shore
That tumbled in the Godless deep;

A warmth within the breast would melt
 The freezing reason's colder part
 And like a man in wrath the heart
Stood up and answer'd 'I have felt'.

The 'eagle's wing' and the 'insect's eye' are the sort of random examples of contrivance in Nature that Paley used to prove God's existence. Tennyson rejects this sort of evidence, finding proof of God's existence in his own inner feelings, not in rationalisations from external Nature; and it is here too that he is to find Hallam's immortality, in his own continued and increasing feelings for his dead friend. It is possible to assume that Tennyson is here rejecting Nature and Science, as well as Natural Theology – if faith is based on the human heart, 'What matters Science unto men, At least to me?' as he asks in stanza CXX. And it is true that this is one of the answers he discovers to his problems in *In Memoriam*, one of the means by which he achieves reconciliation: his intuitions of God's existence and of Hallam's existence make the external scientific universe simply irrelevant. But once Tennyson has found a secure basis for his faith and stopped, as it were, bothering Nature for supernatural evidences, this paradoxically frees him to see Nature in a more positive light. As with the scientific writers the elimination of supernatural preconceptions and emotional cravings from one's approach to Nature, is rewarded by the perception of Nature's ordered organic structure and harmonious patterned processes. So, parallel to Tennyson's discovery of an independent source of strength in himself, is his discovery of an independent stable order in Nature.

Essential to Tennyson's reconciliation with Nature is his acceptance of the idea of continuous change, once he has seen that change as regulated by harmonious laws, and as productive as well as destructive, involving gradual processes of evolution as well as of erosion. This acceptance of natural change reflects a more positive attitude to change in the human world – the 'change' of Hallam from life to death; the gradual change of Tennyson's feelings about Hallam as time passes; changes in the social and political worlds. Even within Tennyson's bleakest picture of change as erosion, there is a hint of the more positive processes that are also going on:

> XXXV
>
> Yet if some voice that man could trust
>   Should murmur from the narrow house,
>   'The cheeks drop in; the body bows;
> Man dies: nor is there hope in dust:'
>
> Might I not say? 'Yet even here,
>   But for one hour, O Love, I strive
>   To keep so sweet a thing alive:'
> But I should turn mine ears and hear
>
> The moanings of the homeless sea,
>   The sound of streams that swift or slow
>   Draw down Aeonian hills, and sow
> The dust of continents to be;
>
> And Love would answer with a sigh,
>   'The sound of that forgetful shore
>   Will change my sweetness more and more,
> Half-dead to know that I shall die.'

As in the very first stanza, Tennyson can only see the gradual processes of Nature as destructive: just as the streams erode the hills, so his love will be gradually 'overworn' by time. The 'long result' of gradualism is only dissolution. But dissolution in one place must mean accumulation and construction in another – while they erode the hills, the streams also 'sow the dust of continents to be'. The 'continents to be' are the first hint of the productive results that may be gradually evolving out of Nature's destructive processes. Similarly, there have been hints of the psychological 'gain' that will eventually and gradually evolve out of Tennyson's 'loss' of Hallam – in stanza XVIII, imagining the burial of Hallam, Tennyson longs to give his own life for that of his friend, imparting to Hallam 'the life that almost dies with me'. But he goes on to add 'That dies not, but endures with pain, / And slowly forms the firmer mind.' As we shall see later, this slow, painful process of formation is precisely Nature's evolutionary method of working.

In order to become aware of the more organic, productive processes of Nature, Tennyson must first see the balance and order that regulate her structure as a whole. To see these, he must have an insight into the hidden principles that lie beneath her surface chaos and destructiveness. As Tyndall says, 'besides the phenomena which address the senses, there are laws and principles and processes which do not address the senses at all, but which must be, and can be, spiritually discerned.'[26] This spiritual discernment is quite different from Tennyson's earlier search for sinister 'secret meanings' in Nature's surface 'deeds' of destruction. He achieves this deeper insight in the famous stanza XCV when he has a simultaneous intuition of Hallam's presence and of a meaningful order in the universe, as he reads Hallam's letters:

> So word by word, and line by line,
>   The dead man touched me from the past,
>   And all at once it seemed at last
> The living soul was flashed on mine,
>
> And mine in this was wound and whirl'd
> About empyreal heights of thought,
>   And came on that which is, and caught
> The deep pulsations of the world,

Aeonian music measuring out
 The steps of Time – the shocks of Chance –
 The blows of Death.

The image of 'pulsations' suggests the heart of a living organism;
the image of 'music' suggests a harmoniously patterned system;
while 'measuring out' suggests a rational regularity that pervades
and structures what seem to be random or 'catastrophic' events:
'the shocks of Chance – The blows of Death'. The chaotic and
destructive universe that Tennyson was so afraid of is seen to
have a deep order underlying and controlling it. Tennyson has
now seen 'the order which pervades the seeming disorder of the
world', envisioned by Science in Huxley's image. As with
George Eliot, 'the great conception of universal regular
sequence'[27] is central to his faith. The images of rhythmic
change that he uses – 'pulsations' and 'music' – are to be echoed
later in Tyndall's descriptions of the organic universe of science:
'This, then, is the rhythmic play of nature as regards her forces.
… Thus beats the heart of creation, but without increase or
diminution of its total stock of force.'[28]

Waves may change into ripples, and ripples into waves, – magnitude may be
substituted for number, and number for magnitude, – asteroids may aggregate
to suns, suns may resolve themselves into florae and faunae, and florae and
faunae melt in air, – the flux of power is eternally the same. It rolls in music
through the ages, and all terrestrial energy – the manifestations of life as well
as the display of phenomena, are but the modulations of its rhythm.[29]

This vision of a stable rhythm underlying the changes of the
universe necessarily involves an acceptance of impermanence
and instability on the physical level – the level of 'phenomena'
and 'manifestations'. Here all appearances are interchangeable
and finally insubstantial, as they 'melt in air'. Tyndall's vision
of transience is foreshadowed by Tennyson in stanza CXXIII,
when he once again describes the geological universe, in
language quite different from his previous evocation of its
dreary processes of destruction:

There rolls the deep where grew the tree.
 O earth, what changes hast thou seen!

> There where the long street roars, hath been
> The stillness of the central sea.
>
> The hills are shadows, and they flow
>   From form to form, and nothing stands;
>   They melt like mist, the solid lands,
> Like clouds they shape themselves and go.

This flowing, melting landscape of insubstantial shadows, mists and clouds contrasts strongly with the heavy 'materialism' of Tennyson's earlier descriptions of geological erosion as a purely destructive process, wearing down the hills into 'dust'. Like Huxley, Tennyson now sees that 'the most obvious attribute of the cosmos is its impermanence. It assumes the aspect not so much of a permanent entity as of a changeful process in which naught endures save the flow of energy and the rational order which pervades it.'[30] Process, not matter, is the final reality.

The symmetry of the pattern of change in stanza CXIII – sea where tree was, street where sea was – is similar to the balanced, rhythmic interchanges of Tyndall's Universe. But this is not all that the scientists have to say about change and process. While on the most abstract level of physics there may be merely an endless fluctuation to and fro between rhythmically recurring similar states of being, on the biological level the processes are ones of growth, the 'evolution' of something new. The 'great Tree of Life', growing and spreading, is Darwin's image for the development of species.[31] Of course it is true that Darwin's theory of evolution differed sharply from the earlier theories of Robert Chambers or Herbert Spencer, in rejecting their naïve assumption of an inevitable 'law' of necessarily progressive development guiding the process. Instead, he explained evolution by the causal mechanism of natural selection, just as Lyell had explained geological change by the causal mechanisms of subsidence and erosion. Nevertheless, any gradualist explanation such as Drawin and Lyell use does presuppose an 'end' towards which the gradual causes are working, a complete species or landscape whose evolution the scientist undertakes to explain by piling up the evidence of minute changes until they accumulate to form a new whole. Thus a kind of teleology is involved in gradualist explanations, the 'end' towards which the processes are working being the 'result' that the scientist chooses to explain or to predict, rather than a pre-ordained 'goal' of the Divine 'plan'. Thus it is wrong to assume, as some critics have done, that wherever Tennyson uses 'teleological' language he is declaring himself to be at odds with the new science.[32] The cumulative working of processes to creative ends is of the essence of gradualism. Even where Tennyson does speak explicitly of the 'one far-off *divine* event, To which the whole creation moves' (*Epilogue*, my italics), it is just as possible to see him as recasting his image of the divine in the language of gradualist Nature, as to see him importing disruptive divine elements into the naturalistic world picture of science.

'Teleological' language also seems to occur in stanza CXXVIII, where Tennyson, turning to the human process of history, in fact declares his dissatisfaction with a model of merely fluctuating changes, as opposed to a progressive and creative evolution:

> No doubt vast eddies in the flood
>   Of onward time shall yet be made,
>   And throned races may degrade;
> Yet O ye mysteries of good,
>
> Wild Hours that fly with Hope and Fear,
>   If all your office had to do
>   With old results that look like new;
> If this were all your mission here,
>
>   . . .
>
> Why then my scorn might well descend
>   On you and yours. I see in part
>   That all, as in some piece of art,
> Is toil cöoperant to an end.

The 'end' here could be the completion of the plan of the Divine Artist; but it could just as well be the completion of the evolutionary processes of Nature. The simile of the 'piece of art' could be operating like the metaphor of the 'Aeonian music'. Just as the 'music' gives a pattern of law to the random-seeming 'shocks of Chance', so the 'piece of art' gives an organic, interconnected evolutionary structure to the seeming fluctuations of history. The evolutionary interpretation seems the more likely, as this stanza occurs after the stanza in which Tennyson gives us his fully-formed evolutionary interpretation of Nature:

CXVIII

Contemplate all this work of Time,
    The giant labouring in his youth;
    Nor dream of human love and truth
As dying Nature's earth and lime;

But trust that they we call the dead
    Are breathers of an ampler day
    For ever nobler ends. They say
The solid earth whereon we tread

In tracts of fluent heat began,
    And grew to seeming-random forms,
    The seeming prey of cyclic storms,
Till at the last arose the man;

Who throve and branch'd from clime to clime,
    The herald of a higher race,
    And of himself in higher place,
If so he type this work of time

Within himself, from more to more;
    Or, crown'd with attributes of woe
    Like glories, move his course, and show
That life is not as idle ore,

But iron dug from central gloom,
    And heated hot with burning fears,
    And dipt in baths of hissing tears,
And batter'd with the shocks of doom

To shape and use. Arise and fly
    The reeling Faun, the sensual feast;
    Move upward, working out the beast,
And let the ape and tiger die.

Here Tennyson has finally recovered his ability to see the productive and creative aspects of Nature's processes. The evolution of the world and of man is described in organic language – 'grew', 'branch'd'. Not only are the processes creative, but they also include and make use of the destructive, chaotic and catastrophic aspects of Nature, as the earth 'grew to seeming random forms, / The seeming prey of cyclic storms.'[33] Here it is useful to remember again Huxley's phrase about 'the order which pervades the seeming disorder of the world'. Not only does order pervade these apparent 'blows of Chance', but they also contribute essentially to the final productive outcome of the whole process. This new understanding of Nature can be imitated by man in his psychological and moral self-development: he too can use the seemingly random, seemingly destructive griefs and shocks of his life to a constructive and creative result, as he is 'batter'd with the shocks of doom / To shape and use'. Man is no longer a 'discord' in the scheme of Nature, but he can harmonise his inner development to correspond with a true understanding of her exterior processes. That understanding involves his ability to predict the future results of those processes – to envisage a 'higher race' of mankind as a possible and desirable outcome. Once he has imagined this result he can to some extent foreshadow it, or work towards it, in the development of his own character into a higher phase of humanity, as he moves upward from his animal origins. As Clifford says, 'we are individually responsible for what the human race will be in the future, because every one of our actions goes to determine what the character of the race shall be tomorrow'.[34]

The organic, evolutionary picture of Nature that Tennyson creates in this stanza contrasts strongly with the dead, mechanical, destructive Nature he described to us in stanza LVI, with her careless and wasteful extinction of thousands of species. He can now see that evolution is the complementary process to extinction, the 'gain' that balances and develops out of the 'loss'. As with the scientific writers, this transformation of his picture of Nature depends on his imaginative ability to see her hidden rhythms, organic structure, and cumulative gradual processes. And also like them, he sees this insight into Nature as applicable to the understanding of the human world, to historical and to personal development. Just as Nature gradually grows into new and higher forms, through seeming cataclysms, and making productive use of seemingly destructive processes, so Tennyson can now see that he has grown through his gradual response to the catastrophic experience of Hallam's death. Time has not in fact 'overworn' or eroded his love for Hallam; instead, that love has gradually grown through suffering into a higher form. This is the end result that he was afraid to 'forecast' in stanza 1. He finally realises this in the Epilogue:

> Tho' I since then have number'd o'er
> > Some thrice three years: they went and came,
> > Remade the blood and changed the frame,
> And yet is love not less but more:
>
> ....
>
> Regret is dead, but love is more
> > Than in the summers that are flown,
> > For I myself with these have grown
> To something greater than before.

So Tennyson has, after all, risen on stepping-stones of his dead selves to higher things. The change of attitude from stanza 1 to here has been gradual, and almost imperceptible – Tennyson has seemed to be undergoing cataclysms and regressions, but all the time, by hidden processes, his love has been accumulating and his character developing. So the 'evolution' stanza, CXVIII, can be seen as a microcosm of the development of the whole poem. The 'seeming-random' structure has an underlying order and direction to it, the emotional chaos of the opening stanzas finally resolves itself into the peace and harmony of the ending, and we can then see that the initial chaos was necessary to the final result. Moreover, stanza CXVIII also encapsulates the parallel developments that have been taking place in the poem, between Tennyson's picture of the scientific universe, and his

emotional and psychological state. Thus, in stanza CXVIII, we
see Nature's evolution, through chaos and catastrophe, to the
higher race, parallelled by man's imitation of the process,
through 'fears', 'tears' and 'shocks' to 'shape and use'. Similarly,
in the poem as a whole, we see Tennyson's actual descriptions
of the Universe evolving from evocations of random chaos and
destructiveness to visions of harmony and productive growth;
and, parallel to this, we see his descriptions of his state of mind
evolving from evocations of fear, grief and shock, to celebra-
tions of his growth. As for the later scientific writers, natural
processes, scientifically understood, provide the central model
for human development.

Tennyson applies his scientific understanding of the ordered
structure and gradual processes of natural law not only to his
personal development, but also to his vision of social change.
This harmony between personal and social change, both
described in terms of evolutionary process, is very clear in the
stanzas describing the third Christmas and New Year:

CV

To-night ungather'd let us leave
This laurel, let this holly stand:
We live within the stranger's land,
And strangely falls our Christmas-eve.

....

No more shall wayward grief abuse
The genial hour with mask and mine;
For change of place, like growth of time,
Has broke the bond of dying use.

....

But let no footstep beat the floor,
Nor bowl of wassail mantle warm;
For who would keep an ancient form
Thro' which the spirit breathes no more?

But neither song, nor game nor feast;
Nor harp be touch'd, nor flute be blown;

No dance, no motion, save alone
What lightens in the lucid east

Of rising worlds by yonder wood.
    Long sleeps the summer in the seed;
    Run out your measured arcs, and lead
The closing cycle rich in good.

CVI
Ring out, wild bells, to the wild sky,
    The flying cloud, the frosty light.
    The year is dying in the night;
Ring out, wild bells, and let him die.

....

Ring out the grief that saps the mind,
    For those that here we see no more;
    Ring out the feud of rich and poor,
Ring in redress to all mankind.

Ring out a slowly dying cause,
    And ancient forms of party strife;
    Ring in the nobler forms of life,
With sweeter manners, purer laws.

In both Tennyson's family life and in the life of society at large, a balance and interdependence is recognised between erosive and evolutionary processes. The 'ancient form' of Christmas celebration, and the 'ancient forms' of political strife, are both recognised as obsolete and ripe for extinction, like the many 'types' that Nature has to destroy on her evolutionary path. The word 'form' is one that Tennyson uses to connect the natural and human worlds – in the natural world, for instance he saw the evolution of 'seeming-random forms'; or the hills flowing 'from form to form'. In stanzas CV and CVI, the extinction of the ancient forms is described in specifically gradualist language – 'change of place, like growth of time, / Has broke the bond of dying use', and 'Ring out a slowly dying cause' – in both cases, the obsolete customs were slowly 'dying' anyway, so that their disappearance is not a sudden catastrophe or shock.

The dying of the old is balanced by the growth of the new, most clearly at the end of stanza cv where Tennyson makes a transition from the personal to the universal by means of the image of the star-rise. Here he links the language of his 'Aeonian' vision of natural harmony, with that of his vision of evolutionary development: the 'dance' and 'motion' of the planets, their 'measured arcs' and 'closing cycle', give a reassuring pattern to the passage of time, while the images of the 'rising worlds' and the 'seed' link this pattern with the concept of productive time-processes. In the next stanza, the structural image of the bells ringing very obviously balances the destruction of the old and the introduction of the new, and the New Year is a similarly obvious image for the beginning of a new and better 'cycle' of time. In society, as in Nature, there is an ordered pattern and an evolutionary direction as 'nobler modes' take over from 'ancient forms'. This parallelism between human development and natural evolution, within a universal balancing of destructive and productive processes, is also well described in stanza cIII, where Tennyson dreams of a journey he makes accompanied by singing maidens:

> one would sing the death of war,
> And one would chant the history
> Of that great race which is to be,
> And one the shaping of a star

Social progress also shares with natural evolution the characteristic ability to assimilate and make use of seemingly 'catastrophic' and chaotic events, on the gradual path to a larger 'end' or result. Tennyson makes this clear in stanzas CXXVII and CXXVII:

> And all is well, though faith and form
> Be sunder'd in the night of fear;
> Well roars the storm to those that hear
> A deeper voice across the storm,
>
> Proclaiming social truth shall spread,
> And justice, ev'n tho' thrice again

> The red fool-fury of the Seine
> Should pile her barricades with dead.
>
> But ill for him that wears a crown,
> 　And him, the lazar, in his rags:
> 　They tremble , the sustaining crags;
> The spires of ice are toppled down,
>
> And molten up, and roar in flood;
> 　The fortress crashes from on high,
> 　The brute earth lightens to the sky,
> And the great Aeon sinks in blood,
>
> And compass'd by the fires of Hell;
> 　While thou, dear spirit, happy star,
> 　O'erlook'st the tumult from afar,
> And smilest, knowing all is well.

This vision of ultimate order in social chaos leads on in the next stanza to Tennyson's conviction that in 'the course of human things', in spite of 'vast eddies in the flood / Of onward time', all is finally 'toil cöoperant to an end'.[35] As in Nature, amid the 'seeming-random forms' and 'cyclic storms', there is an ordered, productive process going on.

　Central to Tennyson's faith in stanza CXXVII is his identification of the dead Hallam with the natural order of the Universe, a distant 'happy star' in the cosmic harmony. Tennyson applies concepts and imagery drawn from the natural order not only to his own inner development and to the development of society, but also to the development of Hallam's spirit after death.[36] Of course, Tennyson's belief in immortality would not be shared by scientific naturalists such as Huxley, Tyndall and Clifford. But what is interesting, and what they would have appreciated, is the extent to which Tennyson *naturalises* the concept of immortality. Far from introducing immortality as a supernatural discontinuity for the confusion of scientific naturalism, Tennyson is at pains to present it as continuous and in harmony with the processes of Nature. While at the beginning of the poem he longs for a personal immortality for Hallam, and is frustrated by Nature's seeming denial of this longing, towards

the end his descriptions of Hallam's state and Hallam's activities
are so similar to his descriptions of the natural order of the
Universe as to make the two nearly indistinguishable. For
instance, in stanza LXIII, Tennyson imagines how Hallam may

> watch me where I weep,
> As, unto vaster motions bound,
> The circuits of thine orbit round
> A higher height, a deeper deep.

Here Hallam first appears as a star, participating in the vast and
measured movements of the universe. And it is the idea of
universal natural law that helps Tennyson to accept his friend's
death, in stanza LXXIII:

> The fame is quench'd that I forsaw,
> The head hath miss'd an earthly wreath;
> I curse not nature, no, nor death;
> For nothing is that errs from law.

The laws that operate in the next world are envisaged by
Tennyson as the same gradualist laws that operate in this
world, and the two worlds are connected by evolutionary
steps, not divided by a catastrophic chasm. This is clear in
stanza XLI:

> Thy spirit ere our fatal loss
> Did ever rise from high to higher;
> As mounts the heavenward altar-fire,
> As flies the lighter thro' the gross.

> But thou art turn'd to something strange,
> And I have lost the links that bound
> Thy changes; here upon the ground,
> No more partaker of thy change.

> Deep folly! yet that this could be –
> That I could wing my will with might
> To leap the grades of life and light,
> And flash at once, my friend, to thee.

Here, though Tennyson has lost sight of the gradual 'links'
connecting Hallam's process of change, he nevertheless implies

that they are there. His vision of Hallam's future state is gradualist and evolutionary, however much this may frustrate his own desire to dispense with the necessary intermediate steps and reach his friend's higher state immediately. This vision of immortality as a natural evolutionary process is continued in stanza LXXXII:

> I wage not any feud with Death
> For changes wrought on form and face;
> No lower life that earth's embrace
> May breed with him, can fright my faith.
>
> Eternal process moving on,
> From state to state the spirit walks
> And these are but the shatter'd stalks,
> Or ruin'd chrysalis of one.

By describing immortality in the language of natural processes and laws, Tennyson not only brings it into harmony with the scientific world view, he also endows it with an agnostic vagueness and mystery, appropriate to that area of the 'Unknowable' which the scientific writers conceded lay beyond and around scientific explanation. This is also true of his attempts to describe God – for instance in stanza CXXIV:

> That which we dare invoke to bless;
> Our dearest faith; our ghastliest doubt;
> He, They, One, All; within, without;
> The Power in darkness whom we guess;

or at the very end of the poem, where God is described in naturalistic, scientific terms of 'law' and 'element' and gradual process:

> That God, which ever lives and loves,
> One God, one law, one element,
> And one far-off divine event,
> To which the whole creation moves.

As Dowden puts it, contrasting Tennyson's attitude to the divine with Browning's 'transcendentalism', Tennyson shows 'a disposition to rest in the orderly manifestation of God, as the

supreme Law-giver, and even to identify him with his presentation of himself, in the physical and moral order of the
universe'.[37] This disposition is beautifully illustrated in stanza
xcv, when Hallam, God and Nature are all involved in
Tennyson's vision of cosmic order:

> So word by word, and line by line,
>> The dead man touch'd me from the past,
>> And all at once it seem'd at last
> The living soul was flash'd on mine,
>
> And mine in this was wound, and whirl'd
>> About empyreal heights of thought,
>> And came on that which is, and caught
> The deep pulsations of the world,
>
> Aeonian music

Tennyson at first wrote '*His* living soul' in line 4 here, in which
case we would assume he means Hallam's soul, and is affirming
Hallam's immortality. On the change to '*The* living soul',
Tennyson commented with disarming agnosticism, 'The Deity,
maybe.'[38]

There are other notably agnostic features of the poem. It has
been pointed out by Basil Willey that Tennyson faces up to the
ultimate questions of immortality and God's existence, virtually
unprovided with Christian supports.[39] We can view the whole
poem as a vast series of experiments, with no Christian 'preconceptions', to determine what we can be certain of in the face
of death. Tennyson, like Huxley, discards tradition and seeks
to base his faith on experimental truth.[40] He does not evade any
of the hard facts of science however much they may appear to
be at war with what he wishes to believe, as in stanza LVI, where
the evidence of extinction 'From scarped cliff and quarried
stone' seems to contradict his wish for natural proof of immortality. This disposition in Tennyson is supported by this
report of his conversation:

spoke of the wonderful variety of forms of life, instinct of plants, etc., told
the story of 'a Brahmin destroying a microscope because it showed him

animals killing each other in a drop of water'; 'significant, as if we could destroy facts by refusing to see them.'[41]

As well as admitting all the hard physical facts of science, Tennyson also shows a scientific, experimental attitude in his willingness to try out different hypotheses in his speculations about immortality. The poem is full of the hypothetical mode – 'if', 'might', 'could', 'seems'[42] recur again and again. Like the scientist,[43] Tennyson tries out various analogies from the known and familiar in his imaginative attempt to form a clear picture of higherto unknown state:

> Could we forget the widow'd hour
>   And look on Spirits breathed away
>   As on a maiden in the day
> When first she wears her orange-flower! . . .

> LXIII
> Yet pity for a horse o'er-driven,
>   And love in which my hound has part,
>   Can hang no weight upon my heart
> In its assumptions up to heaven;
>
> And I am so much more than these,
>   As thou, perchance, art more than I,
>   And yet I spare them sympathy,
> And I would set their pains at ease.
>
> So mayst thou watch me where I weep....

> LXIV
> Dost thou look back on what has been,
>   As some divinely gifted man,
>   Whose life in low estate began
> And on a simple village green....

> XCVII
> Two partners of a married life –
>   I look'd on these and thought of thee
>   In vastness and in mystery,
> And of my spirit as a wife.

In the end, however, it seems to be the analogy of natural process, rather than any of these human analogies, that

Tennyson prefers as a model for immortality, thus bringing it into harmony with the pattern of scientific thought.

Of course, here he is pushing his imaginative vision into an area which the scientific writers firmly avoid. But, as we have seen, they did themselves realise how great a part imagination played in the construction of their ideal vision of order in the natural world. Tennyson also recognises this in stanza CXXII:

> Oh, wast thou with me, dearest, then,
>> While I rose up against my doom,
>> And yearn'd to burst the folded gloom,
> To bare the eternal Heavens again,
>
> To feel once more, in placid awe,
>> The strong imagination roll
>> A sphere of stars about my soul,
> In all her motion one with law;

Here, he sees the vision of 'Aeonian music' and cosmic order, as a product of 'the strong imagination'; but the imaginative vision, like that of the scientific writers, is regulated and controlled by the idea of 'law' – it is no wild and arbitrary fantasy. In fact, this controlled 'scientific' use of the imagination contrasts markedly with Tennyson's earlier frightening 'poetic' vision of a disordered and 'fantastic' universe, in stanza XXXIV:

> This round of green, this orb of flame,
>> Fantastic beauty; such as lurks
>> In some wild Poet, when he works
> Without a conscience or an aim.

Tennyson's law-like vision of the future state is one solution to his problems in *In Memoriam* – but even towards this solution he adopts an agnostic stance, preferring to leave the area of the Unknowable ultimately mysterious, as thescientific writers recommend, and to return to merely human experience for the meaning and purpose in his life:

> CVIII
> I will not shut me from my kind,
>> And, lest I stiffen into stone,

> I will not eat my heart alone,
> Nor feed with sighs a passing wind:
>
> What profit lies in barren faith,
>   And vacant yearning, tho' with might
>   To scale the heaven's highest height,
> Or drive beneath the wells of Death?
>
> What find I in the highest place,
>   But mine own phantom chanting hymns?
>   And on the depths of death there swims
> The reflex of a human face.
>
> I'll rather take what fruit may be
>   Of sorrow under human skies:
>   'Tis held that sorrow makes us wise,
> Whatever wisdom sleep with thee.

Dowden sees this limitation of Tennyson's aspirations to the human sphere as strong evidence of his leanings towards 'the scientific movement'. The very stanza which is often quoted as evidence of Tennyson's complete rejection of science is seen by Dowden as evidence of this tendency:

When dark fears assail him, and it is science that inspires and urges on such fears, Mr. Tennyson does not confront them, as Mr. Browning might, armed with the sword of the spirit and the shield of faith, which that militant transcendental poet knows so well to put to use. Mr. Tennyson flies for refuge to the citadel of the heart:

> 'A warmth within the breast would melt
>   The freezing reason's colder part,
>   And like a man in wrath the heart
> Stood up and answer'd "I have felt".'[44]

For Dowden, it is Tennyson's humanism that makes him more 'scientific' than the 'transcendentalist' Browning, and he goes on to link this humanism essentially to gradualism, again contrasting Tennyson with Browning:

Dutiful activity in the sphere of the practical appears to Mr. Tennyson so much more needed than to seek oversoon for a mystical vision of things divine. No true reformation was ever sudden; let us innovate like nature and like time. Men may rise to higher things, not on wings, but on 'stepping-stones of their dead selves'.[45]

I think that this centrality of gradualism to all aspects of *In Memoriam* is what links the poem most closely to the scientific world view. By separating, juxtaposing, and finally balancing two sorts of gradualism – the erosive and the evolutionary – Tennyson elaborates and refines upon the implications of that world view. His own attitudes to the gradual processes he sees in Nature are very similar to those of the scientific writers – from a heroic facing of facts that seem to destroy his dearest dreams, to an imaginative perception of harmonious law and organic pattern pervading the constantly changing universe. Like the scientific writers, he sees this insight as one that can be transferred to the human world, both as a way of understanding, and as a way of acting, of putting ourselves in co-operative harmony with the processes of Nature. His essentially agnostic approach to ultimate issues also links him with the scientific writers, and his speculations on immortality and on God would be seen by them as fulfilling the poet's legitimate task to 'fashion the mystery' of 'the Unknowable', into suggestive but not prescriptive images.

CHAPTER 3

George Eliot

George Eliot's opinion of Promethean rebellion against natural law is clear from this remark of hers on the 'Prometheus Bound': 'The Prometheus represents the ineffectual struggle to redeem the small and miserable race of man, against the stronger adverse ordinances that govern the frame of things with triumphant power.'[1] Prometheus is not granted any nobility, any tragic grandeur here. His attempt is seen as weakly ineffectual, the race he seeks to benefit as 'small and miserable'. On the other hand, the external structure of law is grandly powerful in the restrictions it imposes on human aspiration. There is a note almost of admiration, as well as of resignation, in George Eliot's description of the 'triumphant power' of 'the stronger adverse ordinances'. The necessity of accepting hard and inflexible external truth is a pervasive message in her novels. But this sense of restriction can transform itself into a sense of participation in a wider structure, as we shall see. The 'frame of things' is a limiting 'frame' to our actions; but it is also a living 'frame' of which we are a part. As the scientific writers saw, the framework of 'law' can be transformed into the structure of an 'organism', once we have chosen to participate in it.

George Eliot's knowledge of and sympathy with Victorian scientific thought is well known – most obviously, there are her relationships with Herbert Spencer and George Henry Lewes; she and Lewes also owned books and articles by Darwin,

Tyndall, Clifford and Huxley,[2] and Tyndall and Huxley were regular visitors to her house.[3] As we have seen, Edward Dowden unhesitatingly placed her as an exponent of the 'scientific movement' in literature; and in 1883, George Willis Cooke commented on her 'Philosophic Attitude' like this:

George Eliot was pre-eminently a novelist and a poet; but she is also the truest literary representative the nineteenth century has yet afforded of its positivist and scientific tendencies. What Comte and Spencer taught in the name of philosophy, Tyndall and Haeckel in the name of science, she has applied to life and its problems... .

Whoever would know what the agnostic and evolution philosophy of the time has to teach about man, his social life, his moral responsibilities, his religious aspirations, should go to the pages of George Eliot in preference to those of any other. The scientific spirit, the evolution philosophy, live in her pages, reveal themselves there in all their strength and in all their weakness.[4]

And indeed, almost every aspect of the scientific world view that I have sketched out can be illustrated from George Eliot's novels, most fully and consistently so from *Middlemarch* (1872). 'Gradualism' is the pervading principle of her art in this novel, which was written 'to show the gradual action of ordinary causes rather than exceptional'.[5] The narrator continually emphasises the importance of gradual, almost imperceptible, change in its effect on character and on action. For instance, Dorothea's disillusionment with her marriage is described like this:

that new real future which was displacing the imaginary drew its material from the endless minutiae by which her view of Mr. Casaubon and her wifely relation, now that she was married to him, was gradually changing with the secret motion of a watch-hand from what it had been in her maiden dream.[6]

Here we catch an echo too of the scientific writers' preference for the hard 'real' as opposed to the flattering 'dream' – this gradual process is one of reduction. Or Lydgate's indifference to Dorothea on his first meeting with her, produces this comment: 'anyone watching keenly the stealthy convergence of human lots, sees a slow preparation of effects from one life on another'. This leads into a more general comment on gradual movements up and down the social scale, 'which are constantly shifting the boundaries of social intercourse, and begetting new consciousness of interdependence'.[7] Here, gradualism is involved also with the idea of organic interdependence: the gradual chains of causes that bring people together are also the links that bind them to each other.

The change that 'are constantly shifting the boundaries' within society suggest a geological metaphor – Lyell spends much time describing the gradual processes of erosion and deposition that alter the boundaries of land and sea. Biological processes of growth and development, equally gradual, are also used metaphorically by the narrator – most famously in the comment on the Lydgate's prospects: 'character too is a process and an unfolding'. Later on, Mr Farebrother, attempting to moderate Dorothea's impulsive belief in Lydgate, makes a similar comment: ' "character is not cut in marble – it is not something solid and unalterable. It is something living and changing, and may become diseased as our bodies do." ' The hopeful possibilities of Will's character and destiny, unfixed and wavering as yet, are conveyed by another such comparison: 'We know what a masquerade all development is, and what effective shapes may be disguised in helpless embryos.'[8] These metaphors are not just isolated effects – they point us to the significance of the whole structure of the novel, the way it charts the gradual growth towards moral health and effective living of some characters (Dorothea, Will, Fred); and the gradual decay of others (Lydgate, Bulstrode). There are no sudden falls or conversions, no 'catastrophic' events. Even when the characters experience shock, a biological metaphor can slow down the process – as when Dorothea discovers the truth about her husband's Will:

She might have compared her experience at that moment to the vague, alarmed consciousness that her life was taking on a new form, that she was undergoing a metamorphosis in which memory would not adjust itself to the stirring of new organs.[9]

The change of attitude is a natural 'evolution', not a sudden discontinuity; the new organs are only 'stirring' as yet, and we infer that memory *will* eventually undergo a process of adjustment to the new form life has taken. The metaphor implies that the 'new organs' have been gradually and inevitably forming for some time now – and if we look back at Dorothea's relationship with her husband, we can see that gradual disillusionment has indeed been leading up to some such revulsion.

Similarly, Bulstrode's shock at the 'catastrophic' revelation of his evil past is imaged as a process of memory being forced to adjust to an inevitable process of natural 'growth' – or more likely 'decay' in this case: 'Even without memory, the life is bound into one by a zone of dependence in growth and decay: but intense memory forces a man to own his blameworthy past.'[10] In these two examples – Dorothea's and Bulstrode's shocks of realisation – we again find the idea of gradual process linked to the idea of beneficial disillusionment, as fantasies are forced to give way to a realisation of the hard but true facts. There is also a hint of the curiously divided image of the mind implied by the scientific writers – on the one hand, mental processes go on involuntarily, by inevitable gradual development; on the other, conscious memory can become detached from and unaware of these processes. Here George Eliot resolves the tension by the natural image of an inevitable 'adjustment' of conscious awareness to unconscious process.

Consciousness can become detached from Nature's reality by creating a fantasy-world for itself – but there is also a different sort of detachment, the objective detachment of the scientific observer which enables him to understand Nature's truth. While George Eliot describes the unconscious development of her characters by metaphors drawn from geological and biological processes, she also presents their conscious attitudes in terms of their approximation to the scientific viewpoint. This is brought out most explicitly in the descriptions of Lydgate's scientific research, which becomes the central moral metaphor of the novel.

In contrast with Frankenstein's research, Lydgate's is described in notably non-Promethean terms. His 'gradualist' ambition is to 'work out the proof of an anatomical conception and make a link in the chain of discovery'. He wants 'to demonstrate the more intimate relations of living structure and help to define men's thoughts more accurately after the true order.'[11] The object of scientific research here is to bring men's thoughts into conformity with the natural order, rather than to disrupt or reconstruct that order in the image of men's thoughts. In this, Lydgate contrasts strongly with Frankenstein, who values science only as a means to 'immortality and power', and who pursues his reseach with very different, if deluded, aims: 'Life and death seemed to me ideal bounds, which I should first break through, and pour a torrent of light into our dark world.' The limitations of the natural order are to be broken through, rather than adapted to. The fact that Frankenstein produces only a deformed monster seems to validate M. Krempe's view of science as something that limits and restricts such daring visions, substituting 'realities of little worth' for 'chimeras of boundless grandeur'.[12] But Lydgate's view of science gives us a third possibility – limiting 'realities' can become the object of an impassioned visionary search for order. Lydgate also wants to 'pour a torrent of light into our dark world', but in a very different way:

The more he became interested in special questions of disease, such as the true nature of fevers, the more keenly he felt the need for that fundamental knowledge of structure which just at the beginning of the century had been illuminated by the brief and glorious career of Bichat.... That great Frenchman first carried out the conception that living bodies, fundamentally considered, are not associations of organs which can be understood by studying them first apart, and then as it were, federally; but must be regarded as consisting of certain primary webs or tissues, out of which the various organs – brain, heart, lungs, and so on – are compacted.... And the conception wrought out by Bichat, with his detailed study of the different tissues, acted necessarily on medical questions as the turning of gas-light would act on a dim, oil-lit street, showing new connections and hitherto hidden facts of structure... . This great seer did not go beyond the consideration of the tissues as ultimate facts in the living organism, marking the limit of anatomical analysis; but it was open to another mind to say, have not these structures some common basis from which they have all started, as your sarsnet, gauze, net, satin and velvet from the raw cacoon? Here would be another light, as of oxy-hydrogen, showing the very grain of things, and revising all former explanations. Of this sequence of Bichat's work, already vibrating along many currents of the European mind, Lydgate was enamoured.[13]

Here, the stronger and stronger light of the scientific imagination – oil, gas, and finally oxy-hydrogen – illuminates Nature's hidden structure, instead of breaking through that structure. The 'holistic' approach to the various organs – 'brain, heart, lungs, and so on' – also contrasts with Frankenstein's inept assemblage of separate organs from different bodies in the construction of his monster.

However, George Eliot does hint continually at a submerged parallel between Frankenstein and Lydgate.[14] The 'lovely anencephalous monster' that Lydgate covets at Mr Farebrother's becomes a fitting image of his beautiful wife Rosamond, who ultimately destroys his hopes of scientific achievement by her selfish demands. But it seems to me that George Eliot is hinting at an ironic *inversion* of the Frankenstein story, rather than a direct parallel. Mary Shelley makes it clear to us that Frankenstein's mistake was not just his Promethean ambition, but also the fact that he allowed his obsessive scientific research to cut him off from domestic affections. He ceases to communicate with his family, commenting: 'I wished, as it were, to procrastinate all that related to my feelings of affection until the great object, which swallowed up every habit of my nature, should be completed.'[15] When the monster created by this morbid one-sided pursuit ultimately kills Frankenstein's beautiful and good wife, Elizabeth, the symbolic significance is clear: exclusive focus on science is destructive of healthy emotional life: Frankenstein has chosen the monster instead of the wife. But Lydgate's choice is different – the wife he chooses, though apparently attractive, *is* the monster; his scientific pursuits, though apparently morbid, require a balance and discrimination that contrast blatantly with the impulsive and short-sighted motives that lead him into marriage with Rosamond. For George Eliot makes it clear that Lydgate's mistake was that he did not apply the same moral and imaginative insight to his emotional life that he brought to his scientific work:

He went home and read far into the smallest hour, bringing a much more testing vision of details and relations into this pathological study than he had ever thought it necessary to apply to the complexities of love and marriage, these being subjects on which he felt himself amply informed by literature, and that traditional wisdom which is handed down in the genial conversation of men. Whereas Fever had obscure conditions, and gave him that delightful labour of the imagination which is not mere arbitrariness, but the exercise of disciplined power – combining and constructing with the clearest eye for probabilities and the fullest obedience to knowledge; and then, in yet more energetic alliance with impartial Nature, standing aloof to invent tests by which to try its own work.

　　Many men have been praised as vividly imaginative on the strength of their profuseness in indifferent drawing or cheap narration:– reports of very poor talk going on in distant orbs; or portraits of Lucifer coming down on his bad errands as a large, ugly man with bat's wings and spurts of phosphorescence; or exaggerations of wantonness that seem to reflect life in a diseased dream. But these kinds of inspiration Lydgate regarded as rather vulgar and vinous compared with the imagination that reveals subtle actions inaccessible by any sort of lens, but tracked in that outer darkness through long pathways of necessary sequence by the inward light which is the last refinement of Energy, capable of bathing even the ethereal atoms in its ideally illuminated space. He for his part had tossed away all cheap inventions where ignorance finds itself able and at ease: he was enamoured of that arduous invention which is the very eye of research, provisionally framing its object and correcting it to more and more exactness of relation; he wanted to pierce the obscurity of those minute processes which prepare human misery and joy, those invisible thoroughfares which are the first lurking-places of anguish, mania, and crime, that delicate poise and transition which determine the growth of happy or unhappy consciousness.[16]

Here we can see the scientific attitude to Nature being set up as a moral ideal. In the first paragraph, there is an obvious contrast between Lydgate's reliance on tradition with regard to beliefs about marriage, and his alliance with Nature in the objective testing of his scientific beliefs. We can usefully remember here Huxley's description of the 'ethical spirit' of scientific advance:

The improver of scientific knowledge absolutely refuses to acknowledge authority, as such. For him, scepticism is the highest of duties; blind faith the one unpardonable sin. And it cannot be otherwise, for every great advance in natural knowledge has involved the absolute rejection of authority, the cherishing of the keenest scepticism, the annihilation of the spirit of blind faith; and the most ardent votary of science holds his firmest convictions, not because the men he most venerates hold them; not because their verity is tested by portents and wonders; but because his experience teaches him that whenever he chooses to bring these convictions into contact with their primary source, Nature – whenever he thinks fit to test them by appealing to experiment and to observation – Nature will confirm them.[17]

But obviously the chief quality Lydgate shows in his research is the scientific imagination – the experimental testing of ideas is one of the ways in which that imagination is kept within bounds, made to work in 'alliance' with facts, rather than providing an escape from them. Like the scientific writers, George Eliot draws a distinction between an imagination that is 'mere arbitrariness' ('arbitrary fancy' in Leslie Stephen's phrase), and one that is limited by scientific values of 'knowledge', 'probability', 'tests' and 'necessary sequence'. Like Darwin, in Tyndall's description, Lydgate exhibits 'observation, imagination and reason combined'.[18] The 'vulgar and vinous' creations of the imagination that George Eliot ironically catalogues here – 'Lucifer ... with bat's wings', 'life in a diseased dream' – could almost stand as examples of the 'unbridled imagination' that Tyndall deplores, which 'roamed through nature putting in the place of law the figments of superstitious dread',[19] before the advent of scientific method. Similarly, the action of Lydgate's imagination, 'combining and constructing', revealing 'subtle actions inaccessible by any sort of lens', 'bathing even the ethereal atoms in its ideally illuminated space', strongly recalls the way Tyndall describes the scientific imagination: 'We can magnify, diminish, qualify, and combine experiences, so as to render them fit for purposes entirely new. In explaining sensible phenomena, we habitually form images of the ultra sensible'; 'besides the phenomena which address the senses, there are laws and principles and processes which do not address the senses at all, but which must be, and can be, spiritually discerned'; 'in their different powers of ideal extension consists, for the most part, the difference between the great and the mediocre investigator'.[20]

But this penetrating ideal vision is always brought back to the test of reality, by which it allows itself to be shaped and changed, 'provisionally framing its object and correcting it to more and more exactness of relation'. The process of adjustment which the conscious memories of Dorothea and Bulstrode are painfully forced to make in one unexpected step, is here going on all the time, as Lydgate's conscious theory adjusts itself continuously to the realities of the processes of growth and change. George Eliot is talking here about a scientist investigating biological processes – but, as we have seen, she uses biological metaphors to describe unconscious psychological processes, and a psychological application is invited by the way the object of Lydgate's researches is finally described: 'to pierce the obscurity of those minute processes which prepare human misery and joy, those invisible thoroughfares which are the first lurking-places of anguish, mania and crime, that delicate poise and transition which determine the growth of happy or unhappy consciousness.' This relates ironically back to the previous paragraph – it is in 'the complexities of love and marriage' that these 'lurking-places' lie waiting for Lydgate, but he is completely without imagination of the hidden, minute psychological processes that will draw him and Rosamond together and stunt the growth of both their happinesses. Equally, he is without a clear grasp on the 'testing' financial facts and consequences of marriage. When he finally has to face these consequences, the narrator comments, 'Having been roused to discern consequences which he had never been in the habit of tracing, he was preparing to act on this discernment with some of the rigour (by no means all) that he would have applied in pursuing experiment.'[21]

Interestingly, the description of Lydgate's research is followed almost immediately by an analysis of Rosamond's state of mind in terms which invite us to compare it with the scientific ideal:

But Rosamond had registered every look and word, and estimated them as the opening incidents of a preconceived romance – incidents which gather value from the foreseen development and climax. In Rosamond's romance it was not necessary to imagine much about the inward life of the hero, or of his serious business in the world.[22]

'Preconceived', like 'arbitrary', is a word of instant con- demnation as far as the scientific writers are concerned: as Tyndall says, 'the first condition of success' in science is 'patient industry, an honest receptivity, and a willingness to abandon all preconceived notions, however cherished, if they be found to contradict the truth'.[23] The 'preconceived notions' (probably religious) are always assumed to be pleasant and self-flattering – like Rosamond's 'romance' here. We might expect Rosamond to be criticised here for an overactive use of imagination, in the construction of this unreal 'romance' – but George Eliot has just established the difference between this sort of cheap fantasy, and the true, scientific use of the imagination. In these terms, imagination is just what Rosamond lacks – she is unable to penetrate beneath surface appearances to the hidden pro- cesses going on in Lydgate's mind, or to grasp the practical facts of his career: 'it was not necessary to imagine much about the inward life of the hero, or of his serious business in the world'. It is this imaginative blindness that later leads Rosamond to see Lydgate's scientific interests as 'a morbid vampire's taste';[24] it is only to a shallow vision that he appears a Frankenstein.

Rosamond is similarly unscientific in her understanding of 'necessary sequence' – the principle which guides Lydgate's imaginative pursuit of scientific truth. After Lydgate has seemed to be disgraced, she comforts herself by associating the impending arrival of Will Ladislaw from London, with the hope that Lydgate will move to London:

she felt assured that the coming would be a potent cause of the going, without at all seeing how. This way of establishing sequences is too common to be fairly regarded as a peculiar folly in Rosamond. And it is precisely this sort of sequence which causes the greatest shock when it is surrendered: for to see how an effect may be produced is often to see possible missings and checks; but to see nothing except the desirable cause, and close upon it the desirable effect, rids us of doubt and makes our minds strongly intuitive.[25]

Once again, Rosamond is rigidly clinging to a 'preconceived notion' based on what is 'desirable' rather than what is probable. Her conception of the world is constructed on 'arbitrary' associations, not on a coherent, ordered vision of natural causation. A similar, and more obviously immoral, disregard of consequences which do not fit in with her wishes can be seen in the way she refuses to accept that it was her insistence on riding that led to the loss of her baby; and in her unhelpful, unrealistic reactions to Lydgate's attempts to economise.

The moral failings of other characters too are seen in terms of their deviation from the scientific ideal. Bulstrode also refuses to accept a coherent vision of causal sequences. Looking back at his past, he excuses the 'bare fact' of his evil deed: 'at that distant time, and even now in burning memory, the fact was broken into little sequences, each justified as it came by reasonings which seemed to prove it righteous'.[26] Bulstrode's 'reasonings' have the preconceived aim of proving the righteousness of his conduct – so reality must be broken up to fit the reasonings, rather than the reasonings being adapted to fit the necessary coherence of reality. We are given a good example of Bulstrode's dubious, self-justifying methods of reasoning when he is left to look after the dying Raffles:

Should Providence in this case award death, there was no sin in contemplating death as the desirable issue – if he kept his hands from hastening it – if he scrupulously did what was prescribed. Even here there might be a mistake; human prescriptions were fallible things: Lydgate had said that treatment had hastened death, – why not his own method of treatment? But of course intention was everything in the question of right and wrong.
. And Bulstrode set himself to keep his intention separate from his desire. He inwardly declared that he intended to obey orders. Why should he have got into any argument about the validity of these orders? It was only the common trick of desire – which avails itself of any irrelevant scepticism, finding larger room for itself in all uncertainty about effects, in every obscurity that looks like the absence of law. Still, he did obey the orders.[27]

But not for long, we discover, when he finally allows the housekeeper to contravene Lydgate's prescriptions. Once again, Bulstrode's 'desire', disguised as valid reasonings, obtrudes itself in place of 'law'. In the case of the wrong to Will's mother, Bulstrode was able to 'adapt' the process of causation to his wishes by breaking it up into small sequences; here, the medical 'uncertainity about effects' gives him his opportunity.

In her analyses of Bulstrode's and Rosamond's thought-processes, George Eliot shows how an unscientific attitude to the principle of natural causation leads to immorality and unhappiness. She is making a more subtle application of the scientific writers' morality of 'consequences', their faith that 'the safety of morality lies ... in a real and living belief in that fixed order of nature'.[28] George Eliot traces the many complex ways in which we fall short of that belief, not only in moments of obvious moral crisis, but also in our most commonplace and habitual ways of thinking: Rosamond's 'way of establishing sequences is too common to be fairly regarded as a peculiar folly'; Bulstrode is plagued by 'the common trick of desire'. Thus the 'inconsequential' thought-processes become part of the 'ordinary causes' that gradually, and consequentially, lead to the crises of Rosamond's encounter with Will and Bulstrode's downfall. The inevitable consequences of inconsequential thinking are clearly demonstrated.

The arch exponent of unscientific ways of thought is of course Mr Casaubon. His research method is in clear contrast to Lydgate's. It is firmly based on a fixed preconception:

all the mythical systems or erratic mythical fragments in the world were corruptions of a tradition originally revealed. Having once mastered the true position and taken a firm footing there, the vast field of mythical constructions became intelligible, nay luminous with the reflected light of correspondences.[29]

The basic concepts of 'tradition' and 'revelation' would be anathema to the scientific writers – and Mr Casaubon holds his theory as if it were a once and for all revelation, a tradition not to be questioned, 'Having once mastered the true position.' Just as Rosamond finds all the details of Lydgate's behaviour intelligible in the light of her 'preconceived romance', so Mr Casaubon finds that his preconceived theory of a preconceived tradition makes all the facts 'intelligible, nay luminous, with the reflected light of correspondences'. The image of 'reflected light' is ambiguous: either George Eliot means that the seemingly intelligible correspondences that Casaubon sees are merely a reflection of his false theory; or that the correspondences mirror each other, creating a false sense of connection: as we shall see, mere similarity is no ground for causal relationship. Either way, the 'reflected light', cast back from surfaces, is in strong contrast with Lydgate's penetrating 'inward light which is the last refinement of Energy'.

The deficiencies of 'correspondences' are made clearer later on:

Mr. Casaubon's theory of the elements which made the seed of all tradition was not likely to bruise itself unawares against discoveries: it floated among flexible conjectures no more solid than those etymologies which seemed strong because of likeness in sound, until it was shown that likeness in sound made them impossible: it was a method of interpretation which was not tested by the necessity of forming anything which had sharper collisions than an elaborate notion of Gog and Magog: it was as free from interruption as a plan for threading the stars together.[30]

The etymological metaphor shows us that 'correspondences' need not imply causal connections. Mr Casaubon's grasp of causation is as vague and arbitrary as Rosamond's – she assumes there is a causal connection between the two 'corresponding' events of Will's coming from London and Lydgate's going to London (London being the common factor), because such a connection fits into her preconceived theory that what she desires will happen. George Eliot warns us that Rosamond's mode of thinking risks an unpleasant collision with the real facts of causation: 'it is precisely this sort of sequence which causes the greatest shock when it is sundered'. But Mr Casaubon avoids any such painful shock by giving his theory no fixed, clear, testable formulation – his 'flexible conjectures' can always be changed. We assume that they are not even as sequential as Rosamond's parody of causal thinking: they do not follow the forward moving 'pathways of necessary sequence' that structure Lydgate's scientific hypotheses. So it is not just that Mr Casaubon's theory is never brought to the test of experimental evidence – the theory never even produces a testable proposition because the loose mode of reasoning does not demand it: 'it was a method of interpretation which was not tested by the necessity of forming anything which had sharper collisions than an elaborate notion of Gog and Magog'. We can contrast this 'method' with Lydgate's: 'that arduous invention which is the very eye of research, provisionally framing its object and correcting it to more and more exactness of relation'. Lydgate's method is also 'flexible' – but his flexibility involves first 'framing' a definite 'object', which can be experimentally tested, and then altered to some equally definite form that relates more exactly to reality. Thus it does not matter that the 'object' of Lydgate's research – the 'primitive tissue' – is mistaken: 'What was the primitive tissue? In that way Lydgate put the question – not quite in the way required by the awaiting answer; but such missing of the right word befalls many seekers.'[31] We can assume that, if pursued, experimental testing of provisional but definite 'answers' would gradually cause Lydgate to 'correct' the form of his question until he found the right answer. But Mr Casaubon's mistaken question, 'What was the original tradition?' is, as we have seen, fixed and unchangeable; while his attempted answers are fluid and nebulous – there can be no reciprocal modification.

But what would have been the right question for Mr Casaubon to ask? or is his research irrevocably condemned by the 'traditional' nature of its mythological subject matter? We can see that there *is* another way of studying tradition, if we look at the way George Eliot herself describes and explains the traditional beliefs of Lisbeth Bede in *Adam Bede*, or of the Dodson family in *The Mill on the Floss*.[32] Here, traditions are seen *historically*, as a natural and necessary part of a particular emotional and social structure; and *humanly*, as the expression of particular social needs. Thus they are intimately related to fact and to experience. It was partly from the German writers

Strauss, Feuerbach and Riehl that George Eliot learnt to look at traditional beliefs and customs in terms of their historical context and their social and emotional functions. Mr Casaubon, we recall, was ignorant of German scholarship; and it is this ability to relate his knowledge to living experience that his research lacks – he disappoints Dorothea's desire for 'a binding theory which could bring her own life and doctrine into strict connection with that amazing past, and give the remotest sources of knowledge some bearing on her actions'. A hint of what such a 'binding theory' would be like is given when George Eliot contrasts Dorothea's fragmentary experience of Rome with that of 'those who have looked at Rome with the quickening power of a knowledge which breathes a growing soul into all historic shapes, and traces out the suppressed transitions which unite all contrasts'.[33] This animating power of the historical imagination (clearly lacking in Mr Casaubon) is very similar to the action of Lydgate's scientific imagination – in both cases, hidden connections must be traced beneath the surface of the apparent. As Tyndall says, 'besides the phenomena which address the senses, there are laws and principles and processes which do not address the senses at all, but which must be, and can be, spiritually discerned'.[34] Mr Casaubon's research, on the other hand, remains on the surface, where everything seems fragmentary, and arbitrarily constructs apparent 'correspondence', instead of finding the deeper causal connections 'which unite all contrasts'. A more profound imaginative insight would have produced at once a more scientific coherence and a more human relevance.

Mr Casaubon's way of conducting his life mirrors the unscientific way in which he conducts his research, as we can see in his letter of proposal to Dorothea:

My dear Miss Brooke, – I have your guardian's permission to address you on a subject than which I have none more at heart. I am not, I trust, mistaken in the recognition of some deeper correspondence than that of date in the fact that a consciousness of a need in my own life had arisen contemporaneously with the possibility of my becoming acquainted with you. For in the first hour of meeting you, I had an impression of your eminent and perhaps exclusive fitness to supply that need ... and each succeeding opportunity for observation has given the impression an added depth by convincing me more emphatically of that fitness which I had preconceived ... . It was, I confess, beyond my hope to meet with this rare combination of elements both solid and attractive, adapted to supply aid in graver labours and to cast a charm over vacant hours; and but for the event of my introduction to you (which, let me again say, I trust not to be superficially coincident with foreshadowing needs, but providentially related thereto as stages towards the completion of a life's plan), I should presumably have gone on to the last without any attempt to lighten my solitariness by a matrimonial union.[35]

Here, too, Mr Casaubon is thinking in terms of corresponden-ces and preconceptions. He interprets the fact of his meeting with Dorothea solely in terms of a fixed assumption that all events are providentially arranged for his exclusive benefit. By the light of this theory, the chance meeting with Dorothea becomes 'intelligible, nay luminous' as a 'correspondence' of her qualities to his needs. All further observation of her is only directed towards confirming a 'preconceived' notion of her 'fitness'. Obviously providential arrangement is, in scientific terms, a false principle of connection. Nineteenth-century scientists saw themselves as struggling to substitute the principle of natural causation for the 'teleological' approach of Natural Theology, which explained all natural facts in terms of their divine adaptation to human needs. Mr Casaubon's attitude to Dorothea reads like a parody of Natural Theology – Dorothea's qualities are beneficently 'adapted' to give pleasure to Mr Casaubon, as part of an overall divine plan.

Mr Casaubon's basic assumption is not changed when he finds that Dorothea has hidden qualities which do not meet his needs – he still assumes her basic function is to serve his purposes, and tries to force her to fulfil this function by getting her to promise to continue his work after his death. Just as his mythological theory avoids any 'collisions' with painful 'dis-coveries' that might force it to be modified, so Mr Casaubon withdraws from any close emotional contact with Dorothea, refusing to investigate or understand those facts of her nature which do not fit into his scheme. There is no chance that his view of the world will become modified by the experience of marriage: Mr Casaubon becomes an embodiment of his own theory, as he rigidly repels any contact with Dorothea's living experience – the ideal closeness of 'relation' that Lydgate's theory achieves with the experimental evidence, by a process of gradual adaptation, can be seen as an analogy of the marriage 'relation', which should ideally be a process of gradual adaptation of preconceptions to the living reality of the other. The 'adaptation' in this case is a changing process responding to a changing environment, as in Darwin's theory of evolution, not a fixed quality created to fulfil a fixed need, as in Natural Theology.

By these analogies between methods of research and ways of living, George Eliot refines Huxley's ideal of a 'new morality' based on experimental truth rather than traditional authority; and Tyndall's ideal of a 'moral culture' derived from the scientist's 'willingness to abandon all preconceived notions, however cherished, if they be found to contradict the truth'.[36]

So far, we have been looking at the many subtle ways in which human conduct deviates from this scientific ideal, and our list could be extended by including Mr Brooke's totally inconsequential, fragmentary thought-processes, or Celia's unimaginative preoccupation with external appearances. But what signs are there of a healthy adaptation of consciousness to experience in *Middlemarch*? The most outstanding is the gradual development of Dorothea's moral outlook, culminating in the way she reacts to the shock of facts that seem to show that Will is in love with Rosamond, not with her:

It was not in Dorothea's nature, for longer than the duration of a paroxysm, to sit in the narrow cell of her calamity, in the besotted misery of a consciousness that only sees another's lot as an accident of its own.

She began now to live through that yesterday morning deliberately again, forcing herself to dwell on every detail and its possible meaning. Was she alone in that scene? Was it her event only? She forced herself to think of it as bound up with another woman's life – a woman towards whom she had set out with a longing to carry some clearness and comfort into her beclouded youth ... . All the active thought with which she had before been representing to herself the trials of Lydgate's lot, and this young marriage union which, like her own, seemed to have its hidden as well as evident troubles – all this vivid sympathetic experience returned to her now as a power; it asserted itself as acquired knowledge asserts itself and will not let us see as we saw in the day of our ignorance. She said to her own irremediable grief, that it should make her more helpful instead of driving her back from effort.

And what sort of a crisis might not this be in three lives whose contact with hers laid an obligation on her as if they had been suppliants bearing the sacred branch? The objects of her rescue were not to be sought out by her fancy: they were chosen for her. She yearned towards the perfect Right, that it might make a throne within her and rule her errant will. 'What should I do – how should I act now, this very day, if I could clutch my own pain, and compel it to silence, and think of those three?'

It had taken long for her to come to that question, and there was light piercing into the room. She opened her curtains and looked out towards the bit of road that lay in view, with fields beyond, outside the entrance-gates. On the road there was a man with a bundle on his back and a woman carrying her baby; in the field she could see figures moving – perhaps the shepherd with his dog. Far off in the bending sky was the pearly light, and she felt the largeness of the world and the manifold wakings of men to labour and endurance. She was a part of that involuntary, palpitating life, and could neither look out on it from her luxurious shelter as a mere spectator, nor hide her eyes in selfish complaining.[37]

Here we see the right way of suppressing selfish preconceptions and adapting one's viewpoint to the deeper connections of seemingly unpleasant facts. Dorothea's 'preconception' that Will loves her is of course right, but when she is faced with facts that apparently contradict it she does not cling to it obstinately, or cut herself off from contact with the whole painful situation in the manner of Mr Casaubon. Instead, like the scientific investigator, she first suppresses personal considerations, and studies the facts carefully and impartially in an effort at clear definition: 'forcing herself to dwell on every detail and its possible meaning'. Lydgate, we remember, was criticised for not applying a 'testing vision of details and relations' to his personal life as well as to his scientific research. And it is to 'relations' that Dorothea next turns, striving to see the facts as they relate to other lives, independently of her own needs and wishes: 'Was she alone in that scene? Was it her event only? She forced herself to think of it as bound up with another woman's life.' Significantly, she is starting to formulate *questions*, questions that gradually change and develop as she tests them against her experience, moving towards a new viewpoint, a final question that will lead on to a new experiment in the light of a different theory: ' "What should I do – how should I act now, this very day, if I could clutch my own pain, and compel it to silence, and think of those three?" '

This is the question that prompts her inspired visit to Rosamond, which eventually brings to light the true facts. Some critics have wrongly assumed that Dorothea acts on a false hypothesis (that Will loves Rosamond) at this point,[38] and therefore the analogy between her moral action and the scientific outlook does not hold up, or is not intended. But her error seems to be more one of fact than of theory – the connecting theory in the light of which she tries to understand the facts, and which inspires her next experiment, is the theory that she is not the centre of events, that she is part of a larger whole whose interconnections are independent of her desires. This organic vision is of course a central assumption of Victorian science. It contrasts starkly with the false assumptions of Mr Casaubon, whose consciousness could only see 'another's lot as an accident of its own'. The organic theory to which Dorothea's wider viewpoint is leading emerges explicitly when she looks out of the window:

Far off in the bending sky was the pearly light, and she felt the largeness of the world and the manifold wakings of men to labour and endurance. She was a part of that involuntary, palpitating life, and could neither look out on it from her luxurious shelter as a mere spectator, nor hide her eyes in selfish complaining.

A number of parallels with the scientific world view are apparent here. As with Clifford or Tyndall, Dorothea's strenuous self-suppression and acceptance of disillusionment have lead her to an illuminated organic vision. This vision of relationship gives rise to an ideal of 'co-operancy' and unselfish participation.

Paradoxically, a conscious effort at detachment eventually enables Dorothea to see her oneness with the unconscious processes of life. As we have seen, this paradox is inherent in the Victorian scientific vision. The objective detachment is combined with a penetrating imaginative search for interconnections and hidden causes – 'She forced herself to think of it as bound up with another woman's life';

All the active thought with which she had before been representing to herself the trials of Lydgate's lot, and this young marriage union which, like her own, seemed to have its hidden as well as evident troubles – all this vivid sympathetic experience returned to her now as a power.

The organic vision is only given to those who are imaginatively searching for it – as Tyndall says, 'without the exercise of this power …: causal relations would disappear, and with them that science which is now binding the parts of nature to an organic whole'.[39]

Of course, the chief exponent of the organic vision in *Middlemarch* is the narrator herself. We have seen how she uses 'gradualist' biological metaphors, and the use of the biological metaphor here – 'She was a part of that involuntary, palpitating life', imaging the whole of human society as one living organism – seems to indicate that Dorothea is attaining the same viewpoint as the narrator. The parallel between the narrator's study of society and Lydgate's scientific study of the human organism has often been noted. His aim is

to pierce the obscurity of those minute processes which prepare human misery and joy, those invisible thoroughfares which are the first lurking places of anguish, mania, and crime, that delicate poise and transition which determine the growth of happy or unhappy consciousness.[40]

This could equally well be a description of George Eliot's aims as narrator. We have seen her 'gradualist' interest in the operaton of 'minute processes', and in the slow psychological 'growth' of her characters. An imaginative penetration into the 'obscurity' beneath surface appearances in order to discover and reveal the 'minute processes' is also central to her endeavour. This appears very obviously in the 'microscope' metaphor through which the narrator reveals Mrs Cadwallader's hidden motivations: 'a strong lens applied to Mrs Cadwallader's matchmaking will show a play of minute causes'. But this 'microscopic' use of the imagination is pervasive in the novel – the narrator always draws a strong distinction between misleading surface appearances and subtle inward processes, as in this passage contrasting the characters of Dorothea and Celia: 'Poor Dorothea! compared with her, the innocent-looking Celia was knowing and worldly-wise; so much subtler is a human mind than the outside tissues which made a sort of blazonry or clock-face to it.' Here we could be reminded of Lydgate's 'imagination that reveals subtle actions inaccessible by any sort of lens'.[41] The microscope *is* only a metaphor, and both scientist and novelist depend in the end on the penetrating power of imaginative insight.

Like the scientific imagination, the narrator's imagination is guided by and looking for organic connections. Lydgate's research is inspired by the theories of Bichat, who

first carried out the conception that living bodies, fundamentally considered, are not associations of organs which can be understood by studying them first apart, and then as it were federally; but must be regarded as consisting of certain primary webs or tissues, out of which the various organs – brain, heart, lungs, and so on – are compacted.[42]

This again is an obvious metaphor for the narrator's viewpoint as she illuminates the interconnections of the 'web' of the social body: 'I at least have so much to do in unravelling certain human lots, and seeing how they were woven and interwoven, that all the light I can command must be concentrated on this particular web.'[43] The interweaving of 'human lots' in the novel creates a cumulative picture of society as organism, as one 'involuntary, palpitating life'. But the 'web' image has a deeper interest, a more complex function. Without the Bichat parallel, it appears at first as an *in*organic image – an artificial tapestry woven from dead pieces of thread. However, the actual word 'web' suggests the organic image of the spider's web; and when the same word is used to describe Bichat's conception of the human organism, it suggests a structure of filaments and fibres within a living body. George Eliot speaks here of 'primary webs or tissues' – 'tissues' again is an ambiguous word that can be applied to artificial 'material' as well as organic 'material'. This implication is brought out by the metaphors George Eliot uses to describe Lydgate's further questioning of Bichat's conception: 'have not all these structures some common basis from which they have all started, as your sarsnet, gauze, net, satin and velvet from the raw cocoon?'[44] The 'web' image could thus suggest the same ambiguities that we found in the scientific writers' concept of 'materialism' – a 'materialism' that could transform itself into 'organism' depending on one's viewpoint.

More specifically, the 'web' image seems ingeniously to combine the implications of the mechanistic 'chain' image and the organic 'tree' image, which co-exist as alternative underlying structures in the scientific world view. As we saw, the constricting 'chain' of gradual cause and effect limits man's powers – but if he accepts this limitation, the 'chain' is transformed into an organic pattern in which he can co-operate, and so transcend his limits in the service of a larger whole. This is exactly how the web-like structure of human interconnection works in *Middlemarch* – those who do not accept its limitations find themselves struggling against a restrictive binding force; those who accept their bonds find opportunities for sympathetic expansion and effective action as parts in the social organism. For instance, the impatient and ambitious Lydgate feels hemmed in by 'the hampering threadlike pressure of small social conditions, and their frustrating complexity'.[45] The 'threads' here are experienced more as a *net* than a *web* – or if it is a web, it is a 'hampering' spider's web, rather than a living 'tissue'. Lydgate does not feel himself part of it. In contrast, Dorothea, by forcing herself to see her experience 'as bound up with another woman's life', attains her guiding vision of society as a living tissue which includes herself. Paradoxically, she has now discovered the 'binding theory' that she was looking for from Mr Casaubon – an organic theory that both binds the parts of her world into a coherent whole, and binds her into the social organism. 'Bound' like this, she is restricted, but she is also attached to what gives her life.

The richly ambiguous use of words such as 'bind', 'tie', 'thread', and 'fibre' occurs in George Eliot's other novels too, most noticeably in *The Mill on the Floss* (1860). When Maggie runs off with Stephen Guest, the action is seen by Stephen as an escape from the 'unnatural bonds' of their other relationships, but by Maggie as a rending of 'the ties that had given meaning to duty'. ' "If the past is not to bind us, where can duty lie? We should have no law but the inclination of the moment" ', she says, when she has resolved to return. She is helped by Philip's letter, which 'had stirred all the fibres that bound her to the calmer past'. This recalls the narrator's earlier nostalgia for the scenes of childhood: 'what grove of tropic palms, what strange ferns or splendid broad-petalled blossoms, could ever thrill such deep and delicate fibres within me as this home-scene?'[46] Maggie's causal connection to her own past is a bond that restricts her, a tie that provides guiding laws, and a living fibre that connects her to her roots. In the language of the scientific writers, the restricting 'chain' of causation also provides us with the coherence and unity of 'law' and the kinship and livingness of 'organism'.

Similar ambiguities govern the presentation of inherited social and racial ties in *Daniel Deronda* (1876). Daniel longs to find out about his origin:

The disclosure might bring its pain, indeed the likelihood seemed to him to be all on that side; but if it helped him to make his life a sequence which would take the form of duty – if it saved him from having to make an arbitrary selection where he felt no preponderance of desire? Still more he wanted to escape standing as a critic outside the activities of men.

Later, this longing is redefined as 'a yearning, grown the stronger for the denial which had been his grievance, after the obligation of avowed filial and social ties. His feeling was ready for difficult obedience.'[47] Knowledge of past origins will give life a law-like 'sequence', which will restrict with its 'ties', demanding duty and 'difficult obedience' – but, however painful such limitation and co-operation may be, it is preferable to the freedom of 'arbitrary' choice, and it makes possible a full participation in 'the activities of man'. The values and the vocabulary of the scientific writers can be heard here in the preference for the sequential as opposed to the arbitrary, and for an acceptance, however painful, of the facts of our 'origin', which will lead to effective, co-operative action. In the same novel, Mordecai speaks of his racial ties and their relationship to past and future in more 'organic' language:

'I too claim to be a rational Jew. But what is it to be rational – what is it to feel the light of the divine reason growing stronger within and without? It is to see more and more of the hidden bonds that bind and consecrate change as a dependent growth – yea, consecrate it with kinship: the past becomes my parent, and the future stretches towards me the appealing arms of children. Is it rational to drain away the sap of special kindered that makes the families of man rich in interchanged wealth, and various as the forests are various with the glory of the cedar and the palm?'[48]

The organic 'tree' metaphor rather than the sequential 'chain' metaphor is very apparent here. It is interesting that when Daniel finally meets Joseph Kalonymos, and learns the truth of his origins, 'he seemed to be touching the electric chain of his own ancestry'.[49] Here the chain, while not organic, is at least dynamic – it has been metamorphosed from a 'tie' that restricts into an energy-giving continuum. The 'bonds' that Mordecai speaks of are further transformed into organic ties of 'growth' and 'kinship'. His feelings of personal interconnection and responsibility to the past and future of his race, are strongly reminiscent of the scientific writers' ideal of self-transcendence through racial oneness. In the words of Edward Dowden,

we have found our deep bond of relationship with all the past, and a vista for hopes, sober but well-assured, has been opened in the future … . In the face of death, joy may remain for the individual through sympathy with the advance of his fellows, and in the thought that his deeds will live on when he is himself resolved into nothingness.[50]

Similarly, Mordecai, 'living an intense life in an invisible past and future, careless of his own personal lot',[51] is reconciled to his own death by the faith that Deronda will carry on the work he had begun. As with the scientific writers, the continuing 'process' is more important than its constituent parts, but the concept of 'gradualism' also gives each part, however small, the possibility of a real and momentous effect on the cumulative result.

This progressive ideal is also present in *Middlemarch*. Lydgate hopes, by means of his reforms in medical practice, 'to be a unit who would make a certain amount of difference towards that spreading change which would one day tell appreciably on the average'. And, more than this, 'He was ambitious of a wider effect, he was fired with the possibility that he might work out the proof of an anatomical conception and make a link in the chain of discovery'. Lydgate fails in his ambition; but Caleb Garth succeeds in his more modest yet similar aim of ' "getting a bit of good contriving and solid building done – that those who are living and those who come after will be the better for." ' As Mrs Garth tells him, ' "it will be a blessing to your children to have had a father who did such work: a father whose good work remains though his name may be forgotten." '[52] Caleb's ideal, like that of the scientific writers, is based on a vision of society as a living organism:

Caleb Garth often shook his head in meditation on the value, the indispens-able might of that myriad-headed, myriad-handed labour by which the social body is fed, clothed, and housed. It had laid hold of his imagination in boyhood.[53]

This is reminiscent of the language in which Clifford expresses his progressive ideal:

we detach ourselves from the individual body ... to identify ourselves with something wider and greater that shall live when we as units shall have done with living – that shall work on with new hands when we its worn-out limbs have entered into rest.[54]

George Eliot's final judgement on Dorothea's life again reminds us of the valuable contribution that individuals can make towards the gradual development of the social organism, through the cumulative effect of seemingly insignificant actions:

Her finely touched spirit had still its fine issues, though they were not widely visible. Her full nature, like that river of which Cyrus broke the strength, spent itself in channels which had no great name on the earth. But the effect of her being on those around her was incalculably diffusive: for the growing good of the world is partly dependent on unhistoric acts; and that things are not so ill with you and me as they might have been, is half owing to the number who lived faithfully a hidden life, and rest in unvisited tombs.[55]

The importance and effectiveness of the 'hidden' as opposed to the 'widely visible' has of course been demonstrated to us throughout the novel, in its 'scientific' exploration of the 'minute causes' that lie beneath surface appearances and interconnect the characters. Here the widely spreading effect of Dorothea's character is imaged not as a web, but as a river broken into many small channels. Though the apparent force of the river is thus reduced, its effect is more widely distributed – 'incalculably diffusive'. The image is at first a little confusing, as Cyrus seems naturally to personify Promethean human power breaking the power of external Nature. But obviously in this context he must personify the *external* obstacles that break the strength of Dorothea's human nature, imaged by the river: 'there is no creature whose inward being is so strong that it is not greatly determined by what lies outside it',[56] says George Eliot, explaining Dorothea's failure to achieve the heroic status of St Theresa or Antigone. So instead of a Promethean victory of force against external obstacle we are given an image of human power restricted and broken by external conditions. The image of the broken river recalls the author's words in the 'Prelude': 'Here and there is born a Saint Theresa, foundress of nothing, whose loving heartbeats and sobs after an unattained goodness tremble off and are dispersed among hindrances instead of centring in some long-recognizable deed.'[57] But, as we have seen, the final judgement on Dorothea goes beyond the pessimism of these prophetic opening words. 'Dispersed among hindrances' is translated into 'widely diffusive'. The 'hindrances' imposed by external conditions provide 'channels' for effective action; the restrictive chains can become a network of effective fibres that help to sustain the whole social organism. Like the scientific writers, George Eliot moves from a vision of the restrictive, reductive external limitations to human aspiration, to a vision of effective human participation within an organic structure.

CHAPTER 4

Meredith

Meredith among the Victorian poets, like George Eliot among the novelists, seems to me to have most whole-heartedly absorbed and accepted the Victorian scientific world view. I find this acceptance more evident in his poetry than in his novels, and particularly in his Nature poetry, where abstract concepts about Nature's structure are fused together with concrete description of Nature's beautiful appearances. In a sense, it is to Nature poetry that science can be most obviously relevant, most akin. For the Nature poet, like the scientist, is dealing with the relation of the human mind to the external, non-human world; both poet and scientist are trying to synthesise the surface forms of Nature with underlying concepts. While this is true of all Nature poetry, Meredith seems especially aware of this similarity – the hero of his poem 'Melampus' is a character who is both scientist and poet in the way he observes and learns from Nature. If we compare Meredeith's Nature poetry with that of his Romantic predecessors, we find that there is an extra emphasis on rationality and objectivity in relating to Nature, a stress on her separateness from man, who is nevertheless her child, and who can learn moral lessons from his conscious understanding of her processes. Conversely, any Romantic dreaminess or subjective ecstasy is discouraged as a productive way of relating to Nature. This shift of emphasis mirrors the attitudes of the Victorian scientific writers.

Meredith's poems have often been called obscure – much of this obscurity is illuminated by comparisons with the scientific writers. In this context of shared attitudes and assumptions, he appears much less eccentric and difficult as a poet.

Meredith mentions scientific writers very seldom in his letters, but, on the other hand, when he does, it is with familiarity, with approbation, and in a tone of tacitly accepting what they stand for. In October 1862 he attended a meeting of the British Association at Cambridge, which he writes of thus: 'Yesterday Huxley had such a tussle with Owen! The thinking men all side with the former.'[1] Owen, as usual, was trying to deny man's near family relationship with the monkeys, thus casting doubt on the extension of Darwin's theory of evolution to include man.[2] At the same meeting Tyndall also spoke to great applause,[3] so here Meredith may have come in contact with him. Writing to his friend Maxse in 1874 he assumes that

Tyndall's Belfast Address you have seen, no doubt. It has roused the Clergy, Fred. *They* warned away from the chief works of God and told confine themselves to the field of the emotions!... . The man or the country that fights priestcraft and priests is to my mind striking deeper for freedom than can be struck anywhere at present.[4]

So he shows himself at one with both Huxley and Tyndall in their battles on behalf of the theory of evolution and scientific ways of thought.

He was certainly at one with them in their admiration for and reliance on the hard facts and truths of science, as is clear in a letter of 1862:

I hold the man who gives us a plain wall of fact higher in esteem than one who is constantly shuffling the clouds and dealing with airy delicate sentimentalities, headless and tailless imaginings, despising our good, plain, strength-giving Mother. Does not all Science ... tell us that when we forsake earth, we reach up to a frosty inimical Inane?[5]

Like Tyndall, he distrusts 'unbridled imagination', fantasy, as a way of relating to Nature; like Huxley, he sees Nature as the only reliable basis for faith.[6] This reliance on 'earth' also formed a bond between Meredith and his friend Edward Clodd, the scientific populariser. In 1886 he wrote to Clodd, telling him that 'When we two touch Earth I see that we are brothers'; and in 1902 he assured Clodd that 'I back your *Huxley* throughout'.[7] referring to Clodd's recently published biography of the scientist, a book in which the author in fact quotes from one of Meredith's poems to illustrate a point about Huxley's thought.[8]

Another very significant association is Meredith's involvement with the *Fortnightly Review*, and his friendship with its second editor, John Morley. He appears to have been a regular subscriber to the *Fortnightly*, he took over its editorship briefly while Morley was in America in 1867[9], three of his novels were serialised there, and several of his poems were first published in it. Now, among the *Fortnightly*'s frequent contributors were Huxley, Tyndall and Clifford, and articles on scientific subjects by Lewes, Spencer and others often appeared in its pages. In fact, the Review gives the impression of standing for a certain attitude or set of assumptions, of which the scientific articles form a harmonious and essential part. Thus Morley, in his 'Valedictory' article, while denying that the *Fortnightly* represented a 'sect', yet admits that there was

a certain indefinable concurrence among writers coming from different schools and handling very different subjects. Perhaps the instinct was right which fancied that it discerned some common drift, a certain pervading atmosphere. People scented a subtle connection between speculations on the Physical Basis of Life and the Unseen Universe, and articles on Trades Unions and National Education; and Professor Tyndall's eloquence in impugning the authority of miracle was supposed to work in the same direction as Mr. Frederic Harrison's eloquence in demolishing Prince Bismarck.[10]

Meredith too felt that the review represented a common purpose of which he approved. In 1866, he wrote to his impulsive friend Maxse, disapproving of outspoken, provocative attacks on the Church, which would only arouse reaction, whereas 'what is being done in the *Fortnightly*, for instance, and elsewhere, is efficacious, and does strengthen, while it increases, the silent band. Let Philosophy sap the structure and work its way.'[11] In this purpose, the scientists, with their emphasis on independence of authority and devotion to hard truth, played an important part. The pervasiveness of science in the *Fortnightly* is also remarked on by Edwin Everett in his book on the Review:

For over ten years, the *Fortnightly Review* carried in almost every issue an article bearing in some way upon religion or upon natural science ... . Although few of the regular contributors were scientists, almost all the contributors to this review ... were agreed that nineteenth-century science was furnishing man, for the first time, a sound basis for social thinking, and that any man who wilfully ignored that basis and took his stand anywhere else was no better than a flounderer, perhaps even a menace to society.[12]

This absorption of science into a system of values can be felt especially strongly in John Morley's own articles on political or literary topics. in which he continually uses the modern scientific attitude as a basis from which to criticise the past, and on which to build a new faith. There are many interesting parallels between Morley's articles and the poems of his friend Meredith.

As Meredith's poems are quite difficult, I have decided to concentrate on only two of them, 'Meditation Under Stars' and 'Melampus',[13] and to give a detailed commentary on each. Between them they span the two extremes of Meredith's vision of Nature: the 'Meditation' considers the whole Universe, and speculates on the possibility of life on other planets, while 'Melampus' takes us into the woods, to observe their smallest biological details, and to understand how they all interact in a harmonious ecological system. One deals with the strange and vast aspects of the scientific universe; the other concentrates on the near and the familiar, as they are illuminated by a scientific understanding.

Although 'Meditation Under Stars' was written later (1888), I shall begin with this poem, as it seems to me to provide the basic outline of Meredith's undertaking as a Nature poet, creating a new, more scientifically-based relationship with Nature to replace the old emotional one. The poem first presents us with the image of a dead, indifferent Nature that appears to be the implication for humanity of the new science, but then goes on to repudiate this way of seeing Nature, and to replace it with a new faith. This faith is presented as the result of 'spirit' and 'love', and on a superficial reading of the poem it would be possible to assume that Meredith was *attacking* the scientific, rational approach to Nature, and wanting to replace it with some 'spiritual' or 'teleological' alternative.[14] But Meredith's new relationship with Nature bears a striking similarity to that of the scientific writers. Like them, he distrusts emotional, self-referring reactions to Nature, and stresses the importance of 'Reason' and 'Mind' in a true understanding of her. The words 'love' and 'spirit' in the poem seem to be examples of the reinterpretation of old terms that I have noted in the scientific writings[15] – representing respectively the unselfishness that the scientists linked with their 'objective' response to Nature, and the imaginative vision that they used to see connecting systems of law underlying the phenomena perceptible to the senses. Like the scientific writers, Meredith finds beauty and reassurance in the interconnectedness of the Universe; he too sees kinship with the 'material' world was as implying our participation in a universal livingness, rather than our alienation from a universal deadness. Moreover, as with the scientific writers, his new picture of Nature emerges from an active, interpretative relationship with her: we must 'read' her to discover her true meaning. Without this conscious, rational effort, we may misinterpret Nature: the scientific writers too stressed the necessity for a strenuous attuning of one's mind to Nature, learning to ask the right questions of her, before she could be understood.

There is an especially close parallel between the structure and imagery of this poem and some passages from Clifford's writings. Clifford, as we saw, found consolation for the loss of his religious faith in a new perception of the beauty of scientific Law, and he expressed this new vision in the old religious terminology. He wrote, 'Every time that analysis strips from nature the gilding that we prized, she is forging thereout a new picture more glorious than before', through the 'new grown perception of Law, which finds the infinite in a speck of dust, and the acts of eternity in every second of time'. He asks whether this new perception may not eventually become

first habitual, then organic and unconscious, so that the sense of Law becomes a direct perception? Shall we not then be really seeing something new? Shall there not be a revelation of a great and more perfect cosmos, a universe freshborn, a new heaven and a new earth?[16]

To me, Meredith's poem represents a stage in this process of readjustment, an attempt to bring it about. At the beginning of the poem, the religious 'gilding' is assumed to have been already stripped off: Meredith himself went through no painful loss of faith, and the reconstructive process was more important to him than the destructive. But while the sentimental picture of the Universe has been destroyed, mankind persists in reacting sentimentally to the new picture, which thus appears terrifying and hostile. The Universe seems indifferent and alien to those who previously saw it as man-centred, as they still take the man-centred point of view. Meredith's contention is that the rational attitude, undistorted by personal emotion, gives us both a new picture of the Universe, and a new way of relating to it, based on the perception of pervading Law, as for Clifford. By the end of the poem, this new perception, at first consciously constructed, has indeed become 'organic', once more a direct emotional response to the wonder of Earth: we do indeed see 'a universe freshborn, a new heaven and a new earth'. Thus the scientific anti-emotionalism, delight in Law, and deliberate, conscious interpretation of Nature, unite to produce the new naturalistic faith hoped for by the scientific writers.

The imagery of the poem, as well as its structure, has a very striking parallel in Clifford's writings. Meredith's central image is obviously the stars. This image is especially appropriate for his purpose, the replacement of old faith with new understanding. The stars have always been thought of as guiding human destiny, or at least as signs of divine power, the outposts of heaven: it is the loss of this idea that makes them at first seem 'cold'. But in the new, scientific scheme, the stars still represent the originating power: their 'fires' were the origin of all life; and in their movements they specially clearly exemplify the universal power of physical law. To emphasise our kinship with the rest of the Universe, Meredith introduces the idea of life on other planets. This idea also appealed to Clifford, and he uses it in a very similar way, also in conjuction with an image of the starry sky:

does it help out our poetic emotion to reflect that these specks are really very very big, and very very hot, and very very far away? Their heat and their bigness oppress us; we should like them to be taken still farther away, the great blazing lumps. But when we think of the unseen planets that surround them, of the wonders of life, of reason, of love that may dwell therein, then indeed there is something sublime in the sight. Fitness and kinship; these are the truly great things for us, not force and massiveness and length of days.[17]

For Meredith, too, fitness and kinship are all important, and he uses the same means as Clifford does to re-introduce poetic emotion and sublimity into the scientific Universe. Both scientist and poet are concerned, in strikingly similar ways, to relate the old human values to the new scientific ideas. Clifford turns to speak of the fitness and kinship of the stars, after he has described his loss of religious faith: 'We have seen the spring sun shine out of an empty heaven, to light up a soulless earth; we have felt with utter loneliness that the Great Companion is dead':[18] this is the 'cold' Universe in which Meredith's poem begins.

Here is the first verse:

> What links are ours with orbs that are
> So resolutely far:
> The solitary asks, and they
> Give radiance as from a shield:
> Still at the death of day,
> The seen, the unrevealed.
> Implacable they shine
> To us who would life obtain
> An answer for the life we strain
> To nourish with one sign.
> Nor can imagination throw
> The penetrative shaft: we pass
> The breath of thought, who would divine

> If haply they may grow
> As Earth; have our desire to know;
> If life comes there to grain from grass,
> And flowers like ours of toil and pain;
>   Has passion to beat bar,
>   Win space from cleaving brain;
>   The mystic link attain,
>   Whereby star holds on star.

The image of the 'shield' gives a hard, metallic quality to the 'radiance' of the 'cold' Universe, and also stresses its impenetrability to question: 'Imagination' is unable to 'throw / The penetrative shaft'. That this impenetrable night sky has a wider symbolic meaning, standing for the death of a whole faith, as does Clifford's 'empty heaven', is beautifully suggested by the phrase 'still at the death of day'. Night is seen as a death, a destructon of the comforting daylight. It is inescapable, 'still' returning: we must always come back to this vision. In other poems, such as 'The Woods of Westermain' or 'The Thrush in February', Meredith also uses night more explicitly as an image of death. This suggests a further meaning here. Night is death, which is similarly inescapable, always recurring. The only lights seen in that darkness of death are cold, terrifying, meaningless. Remaining after the death of hope or of life, the stars represent whatever continues: a hard, bright Truth, an indifferent Nature. There is no consoling 'sign' or 'answer' from this power. Like the Nature of the scientific writers, it does not intervene in human affairs, or communicate with us. But the fault is in those who insist on looking for signs and answers:

> Implacable they shine
> To us who would of life obtain
> An answer for the life we strain
>   To nourish with one sign.

However, the later perception of growth and relation is foreshadowed in the natural imagery of 'grain', 'grass', and 'flowers':

> If life comes there to grain from grass,
> And flowers like ours of toil and pain

The new understanding is implicit from the beginning: the question 'What links..?' implies the scientific 'chain' of causation that connects all parts of Nature. Similarly, the possible 'life' that imagination cannot securely picture is described as a growth towards an understanding of the 'links' between stars, in the attempt to

> Win space from cleaving brain;
> The mystic link attain,
> Whereby star holds on star.

But these 'links' cannot be seen until the right way of approach is found. What the wrong approach is, and what it produces, is made clearer in the second verse:

> Those visible immortals beam
>   Allurement to the dream:
> Ireful at human hungers brook
>   No question in the look.
>   For ever virgin to our sense,
>   Remote they wane to gaze intense:
> Prolong it, and in ruthlessness they smite
> The beating heart behind the ball of sight:
>   Till we conceive their heavens hoar,
>   Those lights they raise but sparkles frore,
> And Earth, our blood-warm Earth, a shuddering prey
> To that frigidity of brainless ray.

It is 'human hungers' that receive no answer from the stars. For a man-centred viewpoint they have no consolation. They are mysterious and unknowable, because the wrong questions are being asked, by the 'sense' not the 'spirit'. 'Sense' here means both a limitation of awareness to outside appearances alone, to what can be 'seen', and a personally emotional response: in both cases the intellect is absent, and the vision is confined to the self. The more this narrow vision is concentrated on, the more remote and unknowable the stars appear:

> For ever virgin to our sense,
> Remote they wane to gaze intense

This describes both their physical distance, the impossibility of any certain, picturable knowledge of them, and their detachment from human concerns, the absence of a personal message in the Universe. These two meanings are united by the two meanings of 'sense', which link the particular scene and its wider symbolic reference. The emotional self-referring approach reacts back on the emotions so that the Universe appears not merely unanswering, but hateful and hostile:

> Prolong it, and in ruthlessness they smite
> The beating heart behind the ball of sight

Eye and heart are directly connected, with no interposition of interpreting Mind. The resulting picture of the Universe and Earth's relation to it, contrasts with the new picture that ends the poem. Both are emotional responses, but the second has been guided by reason, to become 'spirit' not 'sense'. Here, the Universe is felt to be both cold and mindless:

> Till we conceive their heavens hoar,
> These lights they raise but sparkles frore,
> And Earth, our blood-warm Earth, a shuddering prey
> To that frigidity of brainless ray.

That the stars should be thought of as cold, is a typically human-centred delusion, based on a physically-felt contrast with the warmth of Sun and Earth. The coldness is also a metaphorical contrast, an image of the indifference of the Universe, as opposed to human emotions. Earth is a 'shuddering prey', for the stars represent whatever is finally in control, 'immortal', in the Universe, and this power is unfeeling and unconscious, 'brainless'. The absence of human consciousness and feeling has been translated, wrongly, into an anti-human indifference and coldness. Here, there is a difference in the ways Meredith and Clifford use the star image: for Clifford, the initial alienation produced by the scientific picture of the Universe is expressed in terms of the largeness and heat of the stars, rather than their coldness and remoteness. However, a parallel to Meredith's 'cold' Universe can be found in an article by another contributor to the *Fortnightly*, J. Cotter Morison:

The Old is passing away so fast, and the servicable New has not come in. The anarchy is getting fierce, almost brutal. The cold brilliance of science, like an Arctic Aurora, is playing all around us, and fascinating all who have eyes to see. But the clear, beautiful stars send down no rays to warm our hearts.[19]

The second half of Meredith's poem is an attempt to bring in 'the servicable New', and to show us the essential 'warmth', physical and emotional, of the scientific Universe, if it is 'read' with greater imagination.

It may, therefore, seem strange that in the first verse 'imagination' is inadequate to 'throw the penetrative shaft', to gain a vision of the livingness of the Universe. Surely scientific imagination is just what is needed here, with its ability to look beyond the senses, and see underlying connected patterns of law? But for this faculty, and what it perceives, Meredith prefers the word 'spirit' – Tyndall too talks of the scientific imagination as a 'spiritual' discernment. The 'imagination' in verse one is unsupported by intellectual insight, it has not 'the lord of Mind to guide' (verse 4). Tyndall has a similar distrust of such imagination:

We hold it to be an exercise of reason to explore the meaning of a universe to which we stand in this relation, and the work we have accomplished is the proper commentary on the methods we have pursued. Before these methods were adopted the unbridled imagination roamed through nature, putting in the place of law the figments of superstitious dread.[20]

The inability of imagination, as opposed to reason, to deal with the new scientific ideas is also expressed by Darwin. In *The Origin of Species* he is trying to explain how such a complex structure as the eye could have evolved gradually by natural selection. He admits that the explanation at first seems 'absurd in the highest possible degree'. However, 'reason' tells him that numerous gradations in complexity do exist, so 'the difficulty of believing that a perfect and complex eye could be formed by natural selection, though insuperable by our imagination, can hardly be considered real'.[21] Here 'imagination' appears as a conventional and limited faculty, tied to what can be fully visualised: this is how the word is being used by Meredith too.

The life on other planets cannot be clearly pictured in conventional terms. But its possibility can be rationally understood, and a new kind of reason-guided imagination (spirit) can conceive of it, in terms of the underlying living principles that connect all parts of the Universe.

This is how 'breath of thought', in verse 3, is able to traverse the Universe. In the first verse, it had seemed as if 'thought' too was out of its element:

> we pass
> The breath of thought, who would divine
>   If haply they may grow
> As Earth

This initial failure of thought can be explained if we recall the scientific writers' idea of unfathomable mysteries which the human mind is incapable of comprehending, and had better ignore as profitless questioning. But this incomprehensibility is only because the wrong question is being asked, the wrong kind of answer expected. If questions are guided by reason looking for rational order, rather than emotion looking for personal 'signs', they will be answered. This claim is well expressed by Clifford:

By saying that the order of the Universe is reasonable we do not mean that everything has a purpose, or that everything can be explained, or that everything has a cause; for neither of these is true. But we mean that to every reasonable question there is an intelligible answer, which either we or posterity may know *by the exercise of scientific thought.*[22]

This limitation of the kind of questions science can answer is also made by Tyndall when he compares 'the mind of man'

to a musical instrument with a certain range of notes, beyond which in both directions we have an infinitude of silence. The phenomena of matter and force lie within our intellectual range.... But behind, and above, and around all, the real mystery of the universe lies unsolved, and, as far as we are concerned, is incapable of solution.[23]

In his Nature poetry, Meredith seems to agree with Tyndall that it is not profitable to explore the mystery: he does not take

up the position that Tyndall offers to the poets of giving form
to the mystery; instead, he explores the imaginative possibilities
of achieving harmony with Nature by staying within the musical
range of science. The first half of 'Meditation Under Stars'
presents us with the burden of the mystery, if one is seeking for
certain answers and reacting in a purely emotional way. In the
second half an answer is found within the range of scientific
certainty, by approaching Nature with a mind rationally
attuned. So when the right questions are asked, thought is able
to 'breathe' in verse 3, even though going 'beyond our bounds'
to the distant stars. This phrase also suggests that when thought
is unbounded by narrow human concerns, it is free to breathe
and explore. This meaning is reinforced by the alliance of
'love', outgoing unselfishness, to the musing:

> Yet space is given for breath of thought
> Beyond our bounds when musing: more
> When to that musing love is brought,
> And love is asked of love's wherefore.
> 'Tis Earth's, her gift; else have we nought:
> Her gift, her secret, here our tie.
> And not with her and yonder sky?
> Bethink you: were it Earth alone
> Breeds love, would not her region be
>   The sole delight and throne
>   Of generous Deity?

Love directs our attention to our origins, the origins of that
love itself: the Earth from which we have evolved. 'Love' is
especially in harmony with Earth, not only because it originates
in Earth, but because it understands its origin, when 'love is
asked of love's wherefore'. The 'tie' to Earth is a double one,
both physical and interpretative, supporting each other. The
chief result of evolution is the consciousness that understands
evolution, as it was for many of the scientific writers. But once
we recognise our physical link to Earth, we can also perceive
the link, the similarity, between Earth and the rest of the
Universe, and that our 'tie' is not less with the whole Universe,
'with her and yonder sky'. Moreover, if Earth can produce our
understanding love, so can the rest of the Universe:

> were it Earth alone
> Breeds love, would not her region be
> The sole delight and throne
> Of generous Deity?

These lines seem to mean that if Earth indeed had the special distinction of alone producing life and feeling, then the expectations of the searchers for 'signs' would be justified and fulfilled; but in fact Earth is only part of a larger scheme of things, and the controlling 'Deity' must be sought in this larger meaning. The lament for the death of Clifford's 'Great Companion', the earth-centred 'generous Deity', is ingeniously turned by Meredith into a reason for a wider faith in a love spread throughout the Universe.

The roles of 'spirit', 'Mind' and 'Reason' in producing this vision of unity are made clear in verse 4:

> To deeper than this ball of sight
> Appeal the lustrous people of the night.
> Fronting yon shoreless, sown with fiery sails,
>   It is our ravenous that quails,
> Flesh by its craven thirsts and fears distraught.
>   The spirit leaps alight,
>   Doubts not in them is he,
> The binder of his sheaves, the sane, the right:
> Of magnitude to magnitude is wrought,
> To feel it large of the great life they hold:
> In them to come, or vaster intervolved,
> The issues known in us, our unsolved solved:
> That there with toil life climbs the self-same Tree,
> Whose roots enrichment have from ripeness dropped.
> So may we read and little find them cold:
> Let it but be the lord of Mind to guide
> Our eyes; no branch of Reason's growing lopped;
> Nor dreaming on a dream; but fortified
> By day to penetrate black midnight; see,
> Hear, feel, outside the senses; even that we,
> The specks of dust upon a mound of mould,
> We who reflect those rays, though low our place,
>   To them are lastingly allied.

In order to perceive this vision, a deeper insight is needed than the senses can achieve: 'To deeper than this ball of sight /

Appeal the lustrous people of the night.' The stars seem no longer cold, but 'lustrous' and 'fiery'. The vastness of the Universe, 'yon shoreless', is not empty, but 'sown with fiery sails': productive life and movement are everywhere. The false impression of 'coldness' and deadness was produced by the hunger of the flesh: 'It is our ravenous that quails, /Flesh by its craven thirsts and fears distraught.' This distrust of the emotions, and of personal fears, in interpreting Nature was of course shared by the scientific writers. For instance, Tyndall says

Were not man's origin implicated, we should accept without a murmur the derivation of animal and vegetable life from what we call inorganic nature. The conclusion of pure intellect points this way and no other. But the purity is troubled by our interests in this life, and by our hopes and fears regarding the life to come. Reason is traversed by the emotions, anger rising in the weaker heads.[24]

At the beginning of Meredith's poem, these emotions, 'craven thirsts and fears', no longer result in anger against Reason's claims, but in despair at having been forced to accept these claims: the emotions still obscure the rational reaction. Meredith's contempt here for the selfishness of 'our ravenous', 'flesh' and the 'senses', and the way he combines 'love' with 'thought', 'Mind' and 'Reason', strongly resembles the moral value the scientific writers put on their unselfish devotion to Nature's truth, as opposed to selfish, superstitious demands on Nature. This closeness of attitude can be further illustrated from Meredith's letters. For instance, he writes that as far as we are 'independent of our personal emotions ... are we nearing to be at one with Nature in her joyful activity, and our view of her work'; thus there are no terrors in Nature for 'one who has grown to the full development of the brain'.[25]

In verse 4, it is 'the spirit', as opposed to the senses or the emotions, which is able to see the underlying, pervasive life and order in the universe:

> The spirit leaps alight,
> Doubts not in them is he,
> The binder of his sheaves, the sane, the right

'He' is the 'Deity' which exists in more than Earth: the 'sane', rational order of Nature, with its pattern of growth and renewal. Like Clifford, Meredith uses religious terminology to describe his new scientific faith. Through a 'spiritual' perception, human life can thus feel at one with the pervading order of the Universe; but, more than this, order also therefore implies pervading life. The vastness of the Universe, its 'magnitude', is not frightening as it was for Clifford, since it is full of one 'great life': 'The spirit'

> Of magnitude to magnitude is wrought,
> To feel it large of the great life they hold:
> In them to come, or vaster intervolved,
> The issues known in us, our unsolved solved.

The same evolutionary pattern is possible anywhere, may have reached any stage: either life like ours is 'yet to come', and its 'issue' is 'known in us', or life has advanced beyond our stage, to something 'vaster' in which 'our unsolved' is 'solved'. The precise form cannot be known, but the spirit's faith is in the 'spirit' of life, the process: 'That there with toil Life climbs the self-same Tree, / Whose roots enrichment have from ripeness dropped.' This describes not only the organic cycle of growth and decay, which is basic to life, but also the evolutionary process, in which change and diversification is brought about through reproduction and selection, and thus depends on death. We may remember that Darwin uses the metaphor of the tree to describe the evolutionary relationships of species, the course taken by life on Earth.[26] Meredith uses the same metaphor, but more fully. So while evolution may superficially appear random and disordered, it has its own intelligible and necessary laws, a pattern which can be repeated elsewhere in the universe.

This understanding of law and its relation to life, this 'reading', belies the 'coldness' of the Universe. But the interpretation must be guided by the intellect:

> So may we read and little find them cold:
> Let it but be the lord of Mind to guide
> Our eyes; no branch of Reason's growing lopped;
> Nor dreaming on a dream.

Typically for Meredith, Reason is here described by an organic metaphor: it is the 'natural' development for man, the growing crown to the tree of life. The new vision of the Universe is no 'dream', not a yearning of unguided imagination, as it seemed in verse 2 where 'Those visible immortals beam / Allurement to the dream.' Imagination only provides a vague dream, that is impervious to close questioning: only through Reason and the spirit can it be grasped and felt. This repudiation of 'dream' suggests a reaction against the relationship with Nature of the Romantic poets. So in 'Meditation under Stars', by the application of Reason, the 'day' of life and light can be transposed into the 'midnight sky' which can now be 'penetrated'; representing mystery it can be understood, and representing despair it can be lightened, by those who are 'fortified / By day to penetrate black midnight'. As in many of Meredith's poems, we need 'light' in ourselves before we can see the light in Nature. Light is a fairly obvious image of Reason: as the scientific writers pointed out, Nature must be approached with the right rational frame of mind if her rational pattern is to be revealed.

To achieve this insight, we must 'see, hear, feel, outside the senses', for the senses can only be aware of the seeming blackness and coldness, not the pervading law and life: as Tyndall says, 'besides the phenomena which address the senses, there are laws and principles and processes which do not address the senses at all, but which must be, and can be, spiritually discerned'.[27] In Meredith's poem, the 'senses' also mean personal emotion: we must 'see, hear, feel, outside the senses' also because personal emotion only clouds and confines the purity of reason, seeing only the blackness and coldness of mystery and indifference. We must escape from the self-referring viewpoint, and we must achieve a spiritual insight into the hidden connecting processes: then our relative smallness and insignificance in the Universe are no longer a source of despair, for we understand how even the smallest part belongs to the great whole:

> even that we,
> The specks of dust upon a mound of mould,
> We who reflect those rays, though low our place,
> To them are lastingly allied.

This interconnection of the smallest with the greatest in the ordered system was also insisted on by the scientific writers, as part of their 'organic' vision of the Universe. For instance, Tyndall explains how the same physical forces pervade the Universe, so that 'what is true of the Earth, as she swings to and fro in her yearly journey round the sun, is also true of her minutest atom. We have wheels within wheels, and rhythm within rhythm.'[28] Similarly, Huxley connects small and great: 'Living matter differs from other matter in degree and not in kind; the microcosm repeats the macrocosm; and one chain of causation connects the nebulous original of suns and planetary systems with the protoplasmic foundation of life and organisation.'[29]

This connection does not have the effect of diminishing the importance of life: rather it is raised in significance by its participation in the greater whole. And a second effect is that the Universe to which it is connected takes on its attributes of warmth and movement. The scientific 'chain' linking life and matter does not drag life down, but raises matter. As Tyndall and Huxley always insist, it is a misconception to think of matter as cold and inert. What is true of the smallest particles of matter is true of the huge material Universe, as Meredith asserts in his final verse:

> So may we read, and little find them cold:
> Not frosty lamps illumining dead space,
> Not distant aliens, not senseless Powers.
> The fire is in them whereof we are born;
> The music of their motion may be ours.
> Spirit shall deem them beckoning Earth and voiced
> Sisterly to her, in her beams rejoiced.
> Of love, the grand impulsion, we behold
>   The love that lends her grace
>   Among the starry fold.

> Then at new flood of customary morn,
>   Look at her through her showers,
>   Her mists, her streaming gold,
> A wonder edges the familiar face:
> She wears no more that robe of printed hours;
> Half strange seems Earth, and sweeter than her flowers.

The ideas of coldness and deadness are seen to be both inappropriate to the stars:

> So may we read, and little find them cold:
> Not frosty lamps illumining dead space,
> Not distant aliens, not senseless Powers.

Our Reason can interpret them, and can discover our kinship and closeness to them. This feeling of kinship with the Cosmos is, of course, echoed in Clifford's speculations on the stars; and also cited by Dowden as one of the imaginative possibilities of modern science, when he suggests that man's dignity is 'exalted by conceiving him as part – a real though so small a part – of a great Cosmos, infinitely greater than he', and celebrates humanity's 'giant kindred, light, and motion, and heat, and electricity, and chemical affinity':[30] Meredith is here realising that possibility.

The kinship celebrated in his poem is one of origin, and of interconnection in the scheme of rational order: 'The fire is in them whereof we are born; / The music of their motion may be ours.' These are the real 'immortal' powers: the 'fire' and 'music', energy and law. As Huxley puts it, the Cosmos consists of 'A changeful process, in which naught endures save the flow of energy and the rational order which pervades it.'[31] And not only the idea, but also Meredith's imagery can be paralleled from the scientific writings. Our especial connection with this energy as originating 'fire' is well expressed by Tyndall: speaking of the theory of evolution, he maintains that

the hypothesis would probably go even farther than this. Many who hold it would probably assent to the position that, at the present moment, all our philosophy, all our poetry, all our science, and all our art – Plato, Shakespeare, Newton, and Raphael – are potential in the fires of the sun.[32]

Meredith transposes this potential to the similar fires of the stars, and, like Tyndall, derives this wider understanding from an evolutionary understanding of our origins. By speaking of 'the music of their motion', Meredith is using the beautiful old idea of the music of the spheres, but reinterpreting it in the light of scientific understanding. The scientific writers also continually use music as a metaphor for the interplay of physical forces, the ordered movement that pervades the Universe. Thus Tyndall saw the 'Constitution of the Universe' as 'rhythm within rhythm', for everywhere there was the 'rhythmic play of nature as regards her forces';[33] and Huxley sees the particles of matter 'moving with inconceivable velocity in a dance of infinite complexity yet perfect measure; harmonic with like performances throughout the solar system'.[34] So the music is 'ours' in that we inevitably share in the rhythm of law. But there is also a further bond: we are able consciously to imitate the sane harmonies of the Universe once we have interpreted them rightly, by behaving sanely and rationally. In this sense too, 'the music of their motion may be ours'. Tyndall also believes in this possibility: 'The world was built in order: and to us are trusted the will and the power to discern its harmonies, and to make them the lessons of our lives.'[35]

A new emotional attitude to the stars and their relation to Earth is therefore possible. When the guidance of reason and spirit has been accepted, the picture in emotional terms is one of relationship and love:

> Spirit shall deem them beckoning Earth, and voiced
> Sisterly to her, in her beams rejoiced.
> Of love, the grand impulsion we behold
>   The love that lends her grace
>   Among the starry fold.

The pervading order and energy, the 'grand impulsion', is called 'love': like the love in us that comprehends it, it is a connecting power, going beyond individuals. Our knowledge of Earth was transposed to the stars, to make the strange Universe seem familiar. This transposition also has the reverse effect: familiar Earth, by her connection with the vast universal process, seems strange and wonderful. Her strangeness is not frightening, for the living fire and music of the whole have been understood. She is given 'grace' by her share in the universal 'grand impulsion' of love. The new vision of Earth comes with the dawn, a dawn of new hope, contrasting with the night of despair: 'new flood of customary morn' compresses the newness-in-familiarity of the vision, and also contrasts it with the earlier 'Still at the death of day'. Dawn as well as dusk, birth as well as death, are recurrent. The 'wonder' seen in Earth, is the 'spiritual' perception of eternal order, beyond the passage of time and appearances:

> A wonder edges the familiar face:
> She wears no more that robe of printed hours;
> Half strange seems Earth, and sweeter than her flowers.

In the stars, it was their potentiality to originate life that was found wonderful: coming back to Earth, this underlying, originating power is wondered at here too, and is more beautiful than the transitory 'flowers' of the life it produces. Tyndall maintains that 'It is the function of science, not as some think to divest this Universe of its wonder and mystery, but ... to point out the wonder and mystery of common things.'[36] This is what Meredith is pointing out to us at the end of the poem, as he discovers Clifford's hoped for 'new heaven and a new earth'.

Meredith's purpose in this poem also has a close parallel in the writings of his friend, John Morley. Morley hoped for a new rationalist faith, based on a recognition of scientific law. He insists that

It is as mistaken to suppose that this conviction of the supremacy of a cold and self-contained order in the universe is fatal to emotional expansion, as it would be to suppose it fatal to intellectual curiosity.[37]

He goes on to ask,

Why should this conception of a coherent order, free from the arbitrary and presumptuous stamp of certain final causes, be less favourable either to the ethical or the aesthetic side of human nature, than the older conception of the regulation of the course of the great series by a multitude of intrinsically meaningless and purposeless volitions?[38]

And elsewhere he observes:

The countless beauties of association which cluster round the older faith may make the new seem bleak and chilly, but when what is now the old faith was itself new, that too may well have struck, as we know it did strike, the adherent of the mellowed pagan philosophy as crude, meagre, jejune, dreary.[39]

It is this seeming coldness and chilliness that Meredith is trying to exorcise, replacing it with the beauty and warmth inherent in the scientific 'conception of a coherent order'.

'Meditation Under Stars' shows us the new picture of the Universe that Meredith had discovered in science. 'Melampus' dramatises Meredith as discoverer, both scientific and poetic, in the figure of Melampus the physician. Like the scientific writers, Melampus looks imaginatively at Nature to discover the order, the 'music', in her seeming disorder, and he then uses this insight to help mankind. His healing craft is a practical relationship with Nature, based on a rational understanding of her ways. The metaphor of healing is especially appropriate to represent a conscious, harmonious following of Nature, for the healer returns to mankind with his knowledge, applies what he has learnt from Nature to humanity. 'Melampus' is Meredith's most sustained presentation of the harmonious interpretative relationship with Nature that he advocates in all his Nature poetry. Melampus in his researches and his vision of rational order, represents a scientific approach to Nature, but we are also led to connect him with the poet: 'the studious eye that reads ... / In links divine with the lyrical tongue is bound' (verse 14). The metaphor of song connects Nature's and the poet's harmonies: an important similarity between science and poetry is that both are attempts to give form to the seeming confusion of experience. Melampus can be seen as an image of the scientist as poet, using his imagination to construct the beautiful order of Nature; or as an image of the poet as scientist, 'physician to all men', as Keats puts it in *The Fall of Hyperion*.

Melampus's observation of Nature is both 'objective' and 'subjective'. He 'reads' Nature in search of 'knowledge'; but his reading is accompanied by an intense 'love' of what he observes, as we see in the first three stanzas:

> With love exceeding a simple love of the things
>   That glide in grasses and rubble of woody wreck;
>
> . . . .
>
> The good physician Melampus, loving them all,
>   Among them walked, as a scholar who reads a book.
>
> . . . .
>
> For him the woods were a home and gave him the key
>   Of knowledge, thirst for their treasures in herbs and flowers.
>
> . . . .
>
> And this he deemed might be boon of love to a breast
>   Embracing tenderly each little motive shape ...

We have seen that for the scientific writers, and for Meredith, a self-forgetful love of the external world for its own sake was the most productive attitude to take towards Nature. Self-concerned emotions, with their distorted, 'subjective' pictures of Nature (either terrifying or sweetly sentimental) must be replaced by reasoned interpretation, but this rational attitude is not cold, it is always guided by 'love': selflessness, respect for and delight in the object itself, sympathetic insight, receptivity, alertness to hidden beauty – all these ideal qualities of a human relationship are transposed to the relationship with Nature by the word 'love', and each is precisely appropriate to the way Meredith describes Nature, and also to the way a scientist like Tyndall or Darwin relates to Nature.[40]

The love with which Melampus observes Nature's details is not merely asserted, it is created and felt in Meredith's description of

> the things
> That glide in grasses and rubble of woody wreck;
> Or change their perch on a beat of quivering wings

From branch to branch, only restful to pipe and peck;
Or, bristled, curl at a touch their snouts in a ball;
Or cast their web between bramble and thorny hook.
(Verse 1, 1–6)

This way of describing the creatures by characteristic movements – 'each little motive shape, / The prone, the flitting'
(verse 3) – is particularly Meredithian. It is much closer to the
way we do see Nature than any static, pictorial description.
Moreover, it helps to combine the poem's double vision of
Nature (the particular and the general, the surface details and
the underlying pattern): though the 'things' are not named,
Meredith conveys a strong sense of their individuality, a feeling
for their quiddity; yet by this anonymous description of their
movement it is made easier for us to pass from individuals to
the idea of the wood as a whole as an interlocking, 'revolving'
system of movements, diverse but harmonised.

But Melampus is studying Nature not just to discover inter-
relations and a connecting theory, as Darwin was, but as a
physician, in order to find secrets of benefit to mankind. But
the sort of secret he looks for and finds is that of the 'balance' or
'measure' of Nature; the sort of disease he cures is human
disturbance of this balance. His healing can thus be seen as a
metaphor for the moral teaching to be learnt from Nature; his
researches are described like this:

The secrets held by the creatures nearer than we
To earth he sought, and the link of their life with ours:
And where alike we are, unlike where, and the veined
Division, veined parallel, of a blood that flows
In them, in us, from the source by man unattained
Save marks he well what the mystical woods disclose.
(Verse 2, 3–7)

This is the scientific search for our origin in and kinship to the
rest of the natural world; but also the moral search for the way
we are to follow Nature, the lesson that instinctive behaviour
may hold for conscious behaviour, the sort of parallels we can
usefully and reasonably make. The solution to this problem

depends on the careful recognition of 'where alike we are, unlike where, and the veined Division, veined parallel', as well as on the admission of the 'link'. As Huxley saw, the 'ethical process' cannot be a direct imitation of the 'cosmic process'; as Darwin recognised, other factors come into play once consicousness has evolved, which make human social and cultural evolution a different kind of process from natural selection, though it is by natural selection that this process has arisen.[41]

In 'Melampus', the creatures' instinctive behaviour, their unconscious knowledge of their place and their relationships, is described with admiration, as an implied contrast to the confusions and pains of human life:

> For closer drawn to our mother's natual milk,
>   As babes they learn where her motherly help is great:
> They know the juice for the honey, juice for the silk,
>   And need they medical antidotes find them straight,
>
> Of earth and sun they are wise, they nourish their broods,
>   Weave, build, hive, burrow and battle, take joy and pain
> Like swimmers varying billows.
>
> (Verse 3, 5; Verse 4, 3)

We have evolved from an instinctive to an intelligent state, so the instinctive creatures are 'closer' to our common origin. This closeness to Earth gives them a value, suggests that something important can be learnt from them. Meredith does not make a direct analogy between this purity of instinct and the human ideal of conduct. The image of Melampus as physician precludes this, for he is endeavouring by conscious study of this instinctual behaviour to discover the 'antidotes' that he can consciously apply to humanity. Merely telling human beings to follow their own instincts will obviously not help them to find the appropriate medicines.

But Melampus is doing more than merely observing which antidotes instinct chooses. His appreciation of instinct consists chiefly in the rational order and balance that he sees in the interrelated activities of the wood:

all sane
The woods revolve: as the tree its shadowing limns
To some resemblance in motion, the rooted life
Restrains disorder: you hear the primitive hymns
Of earth in woods issue wild of the web of strife.
(Verse 4, 4–8)

The life of the woods is valuable because it is 'rooted': a stability proceeds from the 'closeness' to Earth, and a connection to a firm basis of reality is implied. The word 'rooted' connects the actual trees of the wood, the physical necessities of instinct, and the mental need for a basis of reality and order from which to regulate human conduct. Disorder can no more proceed from this rootedness than the tree's shadow can escape from the tree: invisible but unavoidable bonds connect the physical stability and the idea of order. The essential order seen in the wood expands into Melampus's later vision of harmony and 'measure', and this is the 'cure' that Melampus finds for man in Nature, the warrant for sanity and rational behaviour. In the same way, the scientific writers transpose their faith in the rational order of Nature into a standard for ordered human behaviour.

Melampus's loving search for the secrets of Nature that may help mankind leads to a direct communication from Nature: he is allowed to understand the language of her creatures. The scientific ideal of winning replies from Nature is literally embodied. This gift is given to Melampus when, guided by his rational love of Nature, he has gone against the superstitious prejudices of 'his people':

A brood of snakes he had cherished in grave regret
That death his people had dealt their dam and their sire,
Through savage dread of them, crept to his neck, and set
Their tongues to lick him
(Verse 5, 2–5)

Melampus, unlike the ignorant people, asserts his kinship with Nature by cherishing the snakes. His reaction to the acquirement of his gift is also engagingly rational and scientific:

Melampus touched at his ears, laid finger on wrist:
  He was not dreaming, he sensibly felt and heard.
Above, through leaves, where the tree-twigs thick intertwist,
  He spied the birds and the bill of the speaking bird.
His cushion mosses in shades of various green,
    The lumped, the antlered, he pressed, while the sunny snake
Slipped under: draughts he had drunk of clear Hippocrene,
    It seemed, and sat with a gift of the Gods awake.
(Verse 7)

He carefully takes his pulse, and makes detailed observations of his surroundings – 'the lumped, the antlered' mosses, for instance – to assure himself of the reality of his experience. Once again, Meredith is insisting that his vision of Nature is no transitory, emotional Romantic dream, but something permanent that can be attained by the watchful, scientific reason. The mention of 'Hippocrene' at the end of the verse seems to confirm the reference back to the Romantics. This 'Hippocrene', unlike Keats' in the 'Ode to a Nightingale', does not help one to 'leave the world unseen' or 'fade away' and forget the world, but it leaves one 'awake', observant, watchful.

The results of Melampus's gift, the insight it gives him, are described in terms of a harmony in Nature revealed and responding to a harmony in the observer, just as the scientist can only win replies from Nature if his mind is rightly attuned:

Divinely thrilled was the man, exultingly full,
  As quick well-waters that come of the heart of earth,
Ere yet they dart in a brook, are one bubble-pool
  To light and to sound, wedding both at the leap of birth.
The soul of light vivid shone, a stream within stream;
  The soul of sound from a musical shell outflew;
Where others hear but a hum and see but a beam,
  The tongue and eye of the fountain of life he knew.

. . . .

So passed he luminous-eyed for earth and the fates
  We arm to bruise or caress us: his ears were charged
With tones of love in a whirl of voluble hates,
  With music wrought of distraction his heart enlarged.
(Verse 8; Verse 11, 1–4)

The presentation of Melampus's vision of order as light and sound metaphorically conveys its abstractness: they suggest the abstract essentials of the scientific vision, reason and order, clear light and musical sound. These qualities are united in the image of the fountain, which is used to describe both Melampus's state of mind and what he sees in Nature. The fountain image also reinforces the idea of a connection to deep sources of life. The 'whirl of voluble hates' like the 'web of strife' in verse 4, is the confusion of surface appearances in which the loving understanding sees a basic order: and, more particularly, the fierce 'struggle for existence', in which Darwin could see a balanced interrelation of species, and a connecting, rational, theory of evolution. The harmony revealed to Melampus is on one level the biologist's understanding of the place every species fills in the balance of Nature:

> The pendulous flower of the plants of sloth,
> The plants of rigidness, answered question and squeeze,
>   Revealing wherefore it bloomed uninviting, bent,
> Yet making harmony breathe of life and disease,
>   The deeper chord of a wonderful instrument.
>
> . . . .
>
> In stately order, evolved of sound into sight,
>   From sight to sound intershifting, the man descried
> The growths of earth, his adored, like day out of night,
>   Ascend in song, seeing nature and song allied.
>   (Verse 10, 4–8; Verse 13, 5–8)

But this insight has two other dimensions: the harmony has both ethical and aesthetic meanings. This harmony of Nature leads to an ideal of 'Measure' which is the true 'Wisdom' for mankind:

> Him Phoebus, lending to darkness colour and form
>   Of light's excess, many lessons and counsels gave;
> Showed Wisdom lord of the human intricate swarm,
>   And whence prophetic it looks on the hives that rave;
> And how acquired, of the zeal of love to acquire,
>   And where it stands, in the centre of life a sphere;
> And Measure, mood of the lyre, the rapturous lyre,
>   He said was Wisdom, and struck him the notes to hear.
>   (Verse 12)

In the confusion of human life, 'the human intricate swarm', 'the hives that rave', this Wisdom, this rational ideal of balance, can create order. So Melampus's 'cure' for mankind is both physical and moral, as both

> physician and sage,
> He served them, loving them, healing them; sick or maimed
> Or them that frenzied in some delirious rage
> Outran the measure, his juice of the woods reclaimed.
> He played on men, as his master, Phoebus, on strings
> Melodious.
>
> (Verse 15, 1–6)

Melampus's insight into order gives him an understanding of time – like the scientist, he sees past, present and future bound together by the links of cause and effect, expressed here by the metaphor of seed and fruit – and this understanding is transferred to the human world:

> He knew the Hours: they were round him, laden with seed
> Of hours bestrewn upon vapour, and one by one
> They winged as ripened in fruit the burden decreed
> For each to scatter; they flushed like the buds in sun,
> Bequeathing seed to successive similar rings,
> Their sister's, bearers to men of what men have earned:
>
> . . . .
>
> So passed the luminous-eyed for earth and the fates
> We arm to bruise or caress us.
>
> (Verse 9, 1–6; Verse 11, 1–2)

This application of the understanding of inevitable natural causation, and of the interconnection of present action and future outcome, to the sphere of human morality, was also made by the scientific writers. The scientific perception of harmony in Nature has aesthetic as well as ethical implications. In 'Melampus', the connecting link between the rational harmony of Nature and the aesthetic harmony of art, is the god Phoebus, god of both the sunlight of reason and the lyre of art and 'Master of harmonies' of both kinds.[42]

The metaphor of 'song' is also crucial in making this connection. The underlying harmony of balance in Nature that

Melampus perceives is described as song: he 'heard at the silent medicine-root / A song' and he sees 'nature and song allied', in verses 11 and 13. This song is only heard because he is attuned to it, because he too is a 'singer, though mute':

> his ears were charged
> With tones of love in a whirl of voluble hates,
>   With music wrought of distraction his heart enlarged.
> Celestial-shining, though mortal, singer, though mute,
>   He drew the Master of harmonies, voiced or stilled
> To seek him; heard at the silent medicine-root
> A song
>
> (Verse 11, 2–8)

It is the scientific mind's interaction with Nature, by its expectation of order, that produces song, both harmony and meaning. And both harmony and meaning are also produced by the interaction of this scientific vision with human behaviour:

> And there vitality, there, there solely in song,
>   Resides, where earth and her uses to men, their needs,
> Their forceful cravings the theme are:
>
> . . . .
>
> He played on men, as his master, Phoebus, on strings
>   Melodious
> (Verse 14, 1–3; Verse 15, 5–6)

These harmonious rational and moral interactions can be felt as an aesthetic harmony by a transposition from thought to feeling, as Melampus is able to transpose his insight from one sense to another:

> From sight to sound intershifting, the man descried
> The growths of earth, his adored, like day out of night,
>   Ascend in song, seeing Nature and song allied.
> (Verse 13, 5–8)

Though Melampus is 'mute', though his harmony is 'stilled', though the medicine-root is 'silent', 'song' can be heard: the pattern of his relationship with Nature can be transposed into a pattern of sound. The implication is that the harmonies of science can be 'voiced' by art. Melampurs, through his 'studious' scientific approach to Nature, creates something worthy of and analogous to art:

> the studious eye that reads,
> (Yea, even as earth to the crown of Gods on the mount),
> In links divine with the lyrical tongue is bound.
>
> (Verse 14, 4–6)

A sufficiently complete vision, with 'All senses joined', can comprehend the different kinds of harmony simultaneously:

> All senses joined, as the sister Pierides
> Are one, uplifting their chorus, the Nine, his own.
> In stately order, evolved of sound into sight,
> From sight to sound intershifting, the man descried
> The growths of earth, his adored, like day out of night,
> Ascend in song, seeing nature and song allied.

Meredith often uses this image of music to embody the abstract, scientific harmony of Nature – here he gives an added depth to the comparison, by including the literal meaning of music as a human art form: the metaphor is not just an embodiment, it also suggests a convertability.

In 'Melampus', we find Meredith developing poetic possibilities that lie in the nature of science as an activity of the human mind: the faith in order, the love of objective fact, the search for interrelation. Like the scientific writers, he interrelates scientific thought with human aesthetic and ethical feelings, writing about both at once, within an ideal of natural harmony.

CHAPTER 5

Hardy

Because he usually comes last in studies such as this, there is a temptation to present Hardy's gloomy view of the Universe as the final full realisation of the implications of Victorian science. J.W. Beach, in *The Concept of Nature in Nineteenth-Century English Poetry*, exemplifies this attitude, since he is trying to prove a thesis about the inevitable disappearance of Nature poetry. This is how he fits Hardy in: 'With Hardy, romantic naturism is in full retreat. Thoroughly impregnated with the deterministic spirit of modern science, and with no trace of teleology, he finds nature hostile rather than favourable to man.'[1] As we have seen in the scientific writings, determinism need not imply hostility – it can instead call for co-operation. And as we shall see, Hardy's attitude to Nature is much more complex and contradictory than Beach implies. Rather than fully realising the scientific viewpoint, either Victorian or modern, Hardy seems to me curiously both behind and ahead of his time. On the one hand, he does not attain to the full vision of the Victorian scientific writers, but remains stuck in a destructive, reductive pessimism. On the other, he presses at some of the weak points in the Victorian scientific world view, almost pushing through to a more modern construct, in which theories of relativity, and of the unconscious, would play a part. But his basic allegiance is still to the limits set by Victorian science, however much they depress him, or he tries to push beyond them.

Hardy's sympathy with the scientific culture of his age is clearly indicated by several comments in the biography written by his second wife at his dictation. Though he did not know Huxley well, he admired his cast of mind and character: 'For Huxley, Hardy had a liking which grew with knowledge of him – though that was never great – speaking of him as a man who united a fearless mind with the warmest of hearts and the most modest of manners.' The fearlessness I take to refer to Huxley's resolute facing of the unpleasant truth revealed by science – a quality which, as we shall see, Hardy shares. His knowledge of and sympathy with Darwin is stressed too: 'As a young man he had been among the earliest acclaimers of the *Origin of Species*.' When asked to help a doubting clergyman, he replied unsympathetically, 'Perhaps Dr. Grosart might be helped to a provisional view of the universe by the recently published *Life of Darwin*, and the works of Herbert Spencer and other agnostics.'[2] The influence of Hardy's own early reading of Spencer and Darwin has been pointed out by Harvey Curtis Webster in *On A Darkling Plain*.[3] Hardy was also a friend of the scientific populariser, Edward Clodd, and, perhaps most influential of all, a close friend of the agnostic rationalist, Leslie Stephen, 'the man whose philosophy was to influence his own for many years, indeed, more than any other contemporary.'[4] Stephen himself was friends with Clifford, Huxley, and John Morley.[5]

Stephen, as we have seen, was another proponent of the 'facing up to reality' attitude – 'dreams' and 'fanciful palaces' are to be discarded in favour of hard facts.[6] This attitude is certainly shared by Hardy – it is almost a cliché to say that Hardy saw Nature as imperfect and indifferent. In his poem 'The Mother Mourns', Nature laments that Reason has now exposed her previously covered imperfections:

> – 'I had not proposed me a Creature
>   (She soughed) so excelling
> All else of my kingdom in compass
>   And brightness of brain

'As to read my defects with a god-glance,
   Uncover each vestige
Of old inadvertence, annunciate
   Each flaw and each stain!

. . . .

'I rue it! ... His guileless forerunners,
   Whose brains I could blandish,
To measure the deeps of my mysteries
   Applied them in vain.

'From them my waste aimings and futile
   I subtly could cover;
'Every best thing,' said they, 'to best purpose
   Her powers preordain.'[7]

This could almost be read as Nature's response to Huxley's determination to 'strip off' 'the garment of make-believe' and reveal her 'uglier features'.[8] Here Hardy seems to regret the stripping-off: he could be seen as having reached the first stage of Clifford's process of conversion, when 'analysis' has stripped 'from nature the gilding that we prized', and the picture thus revealed at first 'kills our sense of the beautiful and takes all the romance out of nature'.[9] It seems to me, in fact, that Hardy never makes the full transition beyond this stage to the illuminated organic vision that Clifford projects, though there are fragmentary gleams of it all over his works. Curtis Webster sensibly points out that the gloom and pessimism with which Hardy presents his concept of Nature are merely a matter of personal temperament, and are not necessarily inherent in the science from which he derives that concept.[10]

Hardy's pessimism, however, though partly constitutional, may also be a deliberately assumed stance, part of the agnostic strategy – though he may not move on with Clifford to a glorious vision of Law, he could be moving on with Huxley and Stephen to an ideal of effective action in conformity with real possibilities. Hardy himself answered the charge of 'pessimism' by saying, 'my motto is, first correctly diagnose the complaint – in this case human ills – and ascertain the cause:

then set about finding a remedy.'[11] Making a similar point in the 'Apology' to his *Late Lyrics and Earlier*, he quotes from his poem 'In Tenebris': 'If way to the Better there be, it exacts a full look at the Worst', and goes on: 'that is to say, by the exploration of reality, and its frank recognition stage by stage along the survey, with an eye to the best consummation possible: briefly, evolutionary meliorism.'[12] That an understanding of Nature's deficiencies can move one to moral action is suggested by the poem 'The Lacking Sense'. Here we are told that Nature 'all unwittingly has wounded where she loves', for 'sightless are those orbs of hers' – she is an imperfect and unconscious Creator. But the conclusion is:

'And while she ploughs dead-reckoning on, in darkness of affliction,
    Assist her where thy creaturely dependence can or may,
        For thou art of her clay.'[13]

Knowing Nature's shortcomings and impediments, we are moved to assist her – and the idea of our kinship with her is brought in as an extra motive to co-operation.

While such 'philosophical' poems as 'The Lacking Sense' or 'The Mother Mourns' may give us some insight into Hardy's concept of Nature, they come across as versified ideas rather than products of the imagination. Hardy tries to fix the generalities of 'The Lacking Sense' to a particular scene by the epigraph 'Scene – A sad-coloured landscape, Waddon Vale', and 'The Mother Mourns' begins with a rather more developed piece of scene setting.[14]

But for a greater fusion of particular detail and general conception, in the manner of the scientific imagination, we must turn to the novels, where detail and generalisation are also set within a context of human conduct and emotion. I want to begin by looking closely at a passage from the early novel, *A Pair of Blue Eyes*, in which one of the heroes, Henry Knight, spends some time hanging on to a cliff-face in danger of imminent death.[15] It is a passage that could be seen as a more complex and concrete realisation of the 'facing up to Nature's harshness' idea. To bring this out, I want to compare it to an article of Leslie Stephen's, 'A Bad Five Minutes in the Alps',[16] which uses the same image – Stephen imagines himself clinging to a cliff-face, waiting for death. Stephen's article was first published in *Fraser's Magazine* in November 1872; *A Pair of Blue Eyes* came out in serial form in 1872–3. Robert Gittings, in his biography of Hardy, assumes a direct influence: 'It is pretty sure that some of the realistic detail, in which Hardy described Knight hanging on the cliff-face in *A Pair of Blue Eyes*, was based on Stephen's essay, "A Bad Five Minutes in the Alps".'[17] I am more interested in the possibility that Hardy could be indebted to Stephen for the basic situation and the emotional attitudes it brings out rather than the 'realistic detail' that Gittings mentions. By comparing the two writers, I want to bring out this similarity – both are embodying an aspect of the scientific world view in a similar image; both see Victorian agnostic man in this perilous, cliff-hanging attitude. But I also want to bring out the way in which Hardy's passage develops further the implications of Stephen's article, thus exploiting some of the contradictions and tensions inherent in the Victorian scientific world view.

Stephen's main aim in 'A Bad Five Minutes in the Alps' seems to be to bring out his most essential beliefs by putting himself into a life-or-death situation; at the same time he takes the opportunity to be ironic at the expense of more comfortable beliefs. It is Sunday, and before he leaves the inn on the mountain walk that leads to his accident on the cliff, he has been wearied by a bad sermon consisting of 'theological shoddy'; he tries reading a periodical instead, and is depressed by a controversy about the effects of prayer. Both the sermon and controversy seem to be dealing in unrealities. Against this empty and obsolete 'supernaturalism' is to be set the stark, practical reality of his confrontation with Nature on the cliff, when it is plain that prayer cannot have any effect in saving him, and theology provides quite the reverse of consolation: as he waits for death, a 'hideous fancy presented itself. I contemplated the possibility of awakening to find not that the highest doctrines of theology were false, but that all its doctrines were true.' However, he soon dismisses 'that ghastly night-mare', reflecting that no one really believes in eternal damnation any more. The central question he is thrown back on is, 'What is this universe in which we live, and what is therefore the part we should play in it?' From this angle, the Universe is exposed as hostile and indifferent to man: 'Nature looked savage enough, marking my sufferings with contemptuous indiffer-ence.' More comfortable feelings about Nature are treated as ironically as 'supernaturalism': 'the whole doctrine preached by the modern worshippers of sublime scenery seemed in-expressibly absurd and out of place.' So what is the part we should play in such a hostile Universe, what human qualities will help us? In the end, the only helpful suggestion that comes to him is the memory of rowing in a losing race on the Thames, 'when all hope has departed, and one is labouring simply from some obscure sense of honour.... Even so the effort to maintain my grasp on the rock became to me the one absorbing thought.' A kind of grim determination to keep going, even without hope, is all that sustains the agnostic – we have already seen this quality exemplified in Stephen's earlier reaction to the accident: 'In dumb obstinacy I clung as firmly as might be to the rocks, and did my best to postpone the inevitable crash.'[18]

But what preserves him is not only tenacity, but the ability to remain clear-headed and unemotional: 'a sort of instinctive sense that everything might depend on my retaining presence of mind'. 'Choking back the surging emotions' that shake him, he is able to discover more secure supports, and raise himself to a safer ledge. In dealings with Nature, as the scientific writers insist, one must remain unemotionally observant and rational. However, Stephen is *not* able to retain his objectivity when it comes to his thoughts, though he is able to control his actions. Objectively, he notes the geological character of the rock, 'exquisitely polished by the ancient glacier which had forced its way down the gorge'. But subjectively he is unable to appreciate its smooth lack of footholds: 'A geologist would have been delighted with this admirable specimen of the planing powers of nature; I felt, I must confess, rather inclined to curse geology and glaciers.' Personal emotion cannot be kept out: 'At times, nature itself became an object of antipathy, and I felt a kind of personal dislike to gravitation and the laws of motion.' Similarly, Hardy's Knight finds himself on the subjective receiving end of geological and physical facts he had previously studied objectively. Stephen, in the grip of his subjective emotions, is tortured by 'wild and tyrannous imaginings'. He focuses on one especial 'pinnacle of black rock': 'it looked like a grim fiend calmly frowning upon my agony. I hated it, and yet had an unpleasant sense that my hatred could do it no harm'; it is 'immoveable, scornful, and eternal'.[19]

What is important here, with a view to comparison with Hardy, is that it is quite clear from the context that this characterisation of Nature is the product of 'wild and tyrannous imaginings', caused by the particular subjective angle of someone hanging on a cliff in fear of his life. Stephen's 'personal dislike' towards 'gravitation and the laws of motion' is set up as faintly absurd. The point he is trying to bring over is Nature's absolute independence of and unresponsiveness to human emotion – 'my hatred could do it no harm'. Prayer has no effect here. He personifies the pinnacle of rock, but it is quite clear that this is the projection of a frightened mind: like the metaphorical use of religious language by the scientific writers, the personification is done 'consciously and above board'.[20] Stephen points out that he 'was at once the actor and spectator of a terrible drama.... My double character enabled me at once to realise the full bitterness of my emotions, and to record them with ineffaceable accuracy.' The careful distinction of objective and subjective is very much in the spirit of the scientific world view. So Stephen is not saying that his characterisation of Nature – 'Nature looked savage enough, marking my sufferings with contemptuous indifference' – is the *truth*, as opposed to the benevolent Nature of the 'worshippers of sublime scenery'.[21] He is asking Nature worshippers to try a different perspective, from which their assumptions will appear inadequate and absurd – subjective projections, just like his own 'imaginings' here. This is the polemical purpose of the anthropomorphic description of Nature here; but it has an interesting artistic side-effect. By making clear the subjectivity of his viewpoint, Stephen is able to use language and imagery deriving from an anthropomorphic concept of Nature, without at the same time abandoning or concealing his belief in Nature's unconscious indifference. This is an opening that Hardy exploits to the full.

Stephen's final rescue is a complete anticlimax. He resolves to attempt a jump to safety, slips, falls – but there turns out to have been a safe ledge beneath him all the time. He remembers now that he had noticed the ledge before – this exonerates him from the blame of having made a dangerous mistake in choosing to cross the cliff in the first place. The accident is in no way his fault, unlike the accident that befalls Knight, as we shall see. We are not allowed to see Stephen's accident as an inevitable result of taking dangerous agnostic paths, as he imagines the preacher of the sermon would see it. The tension is further relaxed when he admits that 'the foregoing narrative is without even a foundation in fact'.[22] This makes us feel that mankind's predicament is not really as grim as Stephen has been making out – the cliff-hanging position was, as we suspected, merely assumed for the sake of argument. Hardy provides no such easy escape route, though there is a similarity between the endings of Stephen's and Knight's ordeals in that in both cases rescue comes at the moment when the tenacious will is relaxed, and all is assumed to be lost. One final point to be made about Stephen's whole choice of scenario is that he has chosen to confront *inanimate* Nature here: rocks, which are among the most obviously 'material' parts of the Universe; and the physical laws of gravitation and motion, which govern the behaviour of matter. Here we have, as it were, the bare bones of Nature revealed, not only clothes but flesh stripped off. Stephen does not stress our kinship with and derivation from this inanimate world – this is an aspect of the situation which Hardy develops – but he does imply that we are conditioned by its laws.

In *A Pair of Blue Eyes*, Knight's experience on the cliff is not set up in ironical contrast to the attitudes of those who give sermons or believe in prayers. If there is an ironical contrast, it is with Knight's own previous experiences and way of life – but it is important to notice that the irony does not invalidate his previous attitudes. He is forced painfully to recognise the power both of inanimate Nature and of his own subjectivity – but Hardy does not let this cancel out the value of his strong, objective rationality. We must look first at the way Knight is described when he first appears in the book.[23] The setting is urban: Bede's Inn in London. Stephen Smith, the other hero of the book, approaches him through a courtyard containing a sycamore tree, 'the thick coat of soot upon its branches, hanging underneath them in flakes, as in a chimney.... Within the railings is a flower garden of respectable dahlias and chrysanthemums, where a man is sweeping the leaves from the grass.' Nature here is subdued, imprisoned and controlled by man. This impression is continued inside Knight's room:

An aquarium stood in the window. It was a dull parallelopipedon enough for living creatures at most hours of the day; but for a few minutes in the evening, as now, an errant, kindly ray lighted up and warmed the little world therein, when the many-coloured zoophytes opened out and put forth their arms, the weeds acquired a rich transparency, the shells gleamed of a more golden yellow, and the timid community expressed gladness more plainly than in words.

We learn later that Knight is an amateur geologist – presumably he also goes in for marine biology. The aquarium here, in which Nature is controlled and contained for observation, is in obvious ironic contrast with the untamed sea that later lashes the foot of the cliff, waiting to devour Knight if he should fall; and the imprisoned zoophytes prefigure the fossil trilobite that will so coldly stare him in the eyes as he hangs in front of it, reduced to its level. But Knight, as we first meet him, is no monster of cold rationality, though he does view life as a detached observer and his face is 'getting sicklied o'er by the unmistakeable pale cast'. But his mouth and eyes still appear 'younger and fresher than the brow and face which they belonged to': 'a dozen years of hard reading' have not dulled his eyes, only given 'a quietness to their gaze which suited them well'; and his mouth only has 'a chronic aspect of impassivity' because its 'real expression' is concealed by his beard – he looks up with a smile when Stephen Smith comes in. His kindly affection for his younger friend could be mirrored in the 'kindly ray' that occasionally transfigures the dull aquarium in his room. The 'Nature' that Knight observes is also his own 'nature': later, on the cliff, the uncontrolled Nature that assaults him can similarly be seen as a reflection of his own wilder passion for Elfride, the heroine, which assaults his usual impassivity. But Hardy is not simply disapproving the scientific objectivity that Knight has here, or setting it up to be ironically demolished later – though apparently 'dull', it has its own grace, and the forces that seek to destroy it on the cliff would be destroying something valuable.

To return to Bede's Inn: we discover that Knight earns his living as a journalist and critic, and we could see him as a portrait of Leslie Stephen, except that Hardy had not yet met Stephen at this time. He is usually taken to be modelled on Hardy's friend Horace Moule, but Robert Gittings disputes this, and finds Hardy himself a more likely model.[24] In any event, we can see him as a very consciously intelligent, objective, scientific agnostic. Later in the book,[25] as Knight sits with Elfride on the cliffs, he shows off his scientific knowledge:

'Over that edge,' said Knight, 'where nothing but vacancy appears, is a moving compact mass. The wind strikes the surface of the rock, runs up it, rises like a fountain to a height far above our heads, curls over us in an arch, and disperses there – as perfect as the Niagara Falls – but rising instead of falling, and air instead of water.'

This is the sort of observation that Tyndall might make in the Alps, using his knowledge of the laws of physics and his scientific imagination to visualise the invisible movements of the air: for instance, he sees in the cloud formation 'visible symbols which enabled us to understand what was going on in the invisible air'.[26] As there are no clouds here to assist the visualisation, Knight uses a stone that he throws over the cliff. He then formulates the further hypothesis that there must also be a 'little backward current' downwards near the surface, and leans over the protecting bank to find out. Proving the truth of his hypothesis, the wind sucks his hat over the cliff, and he follows it. It is Knight's scientific curiosity that leads to the accident:

Haggard cliffs, of every ugly altitude, are as common as sea-fowl along the line of coast between Exmoor and Land's End; but this outflanked them all. Their summits are not safe places for scientific experiment on the principles of air-currents, as Knight had now found, to his dismay.

Knight had forgotten that he was an actor as well as an observer in this scene: his knowledge of the laws of physics, which should have been applied to his own conduct and kept him away from the cliff, has in fact put him in the power of those laws. Hardy is using science as a symbol of excessive detachment and objectivity: Knight's objective detachment from life is about to be shattered by his subjective love for Elfride. On the other hand, the retribution that befalls Knight shows Hardy's sympathy with the scientific world view: that Nature is mercilessly powerful over man if he is careless is a constant theme with tough-minded agnostics like Stephen or Huxley.

Hardy develops more strongly than Stephen the fact that it is *inanimate* Nature who is man's antagonist in this scene. It is as if Knight has slipped over the boundary dividing the living from the not-living:

Between the turf-covered slope and the gigantic perpendicular rock intervened a weather-worn series of jagged edges, forming a face yet steeper than the former slope. As he slowly slid inch by inch upon these, Knight made a last desperate dash at the lowest tuft of vegetation – the last outlying knot of starved herbage ere the rock appeared in all its bareness.

Below the rock, at the foot of the cliff, is the sea. A model of regression down the evolutionary scale has been set up, from humanity (usually) standing on the cliff-top, down through plant life, inanimate rock, to original chaos and formlessness. On the psychological level, Knight could be seen as sliding backwards from his conscious, objective pinnacle, towards more primitive states of mind. Hardy takes up and develops this idea of a movement backwards through time as well as downwards through space:

> He reclined hand in hand with the world in its infancy. Not a blade, not an insect, which spoke of the present, was between him and the past. The inveterate antagonism of these black precipices to all strugglers for life is in no way more forcibly suggested than by the paucity of tufts of grass, lichens, or confervae on their outermost ledges.

Nature has certainly been stripped bare of any pleasant covering here: the thin veneer of organic life rests on this dark unliving structure, both physically and historically. Hardy brings the evolutionary theme into sudden focus by introducing the trilobite:

> opposite Knight's eyes was an imbedded fossil, standing forth in low relief from the rock. It was a creature with eyes. The eyes, dead and turned to stone, were even now regarding him. It was one of the early crustaceans called Trilobites. Separated by millions of years in their lives, Knight and this underling seemed to have met in their death. It was the single instance within reach of his vision of anything that had ever been alive and had had a body to save, as he himself had now.
>
> The creature represented but a low type of animal existence, for never in their vernal years had the plains indicated by these numberless slaty layers been traversed by an intelligence worthy of the name. Zoophytes, mollusca, shell-fish, were the highest developments of those ancient dates. The immense lapses of time each formation represented had known nothing of the dignity of man. They were grand times, but they were mean times too, and mean were their relics. He was to be with the small in his death.
>
> Knight was a geologist, and such is the supremacy of habit over occasion, as a pioneer of the thoughts of men, that at this dreadful juncture his mind found time to take in, by a momentary sweep, the varied scenes that had had their day between this creature's epoch and his own. There is no place like a cleft landscape for bringing home such imaginings as these.
>
> Time closed up like a fan before him. He saw himself at one extremity of the years, face to face with the beginning and all the intermediate centuries simultaneously. Fierce men, clothed in the hides of beasts, and carrying, for

defence and attack, huge clubs and pointed spears, rose from the rock, like the phantoms before Macbeth. They lived in hollows, woods, and mud huts – perhaps in caves of the neighbouring rocks. Behind them stood an earlier band. No man was there. Huge elephantine forms, the mastodon, the hippopotamus, the tapir, antelopes of monstrous size, the megatherium, and the mylodon – all, for the moment, in juxtaposition. Further back, and overlapped by these, were perched huge-billed birds and swinish creatures as large as horses. Still more shadowy were the sinister crocodilian outlines – alligators and other uncouth shapes, culminating in the colossal lizard, the iguanodon. Folded behind were dragon forms and clouds of flying reptiles: still underneath were fishy beings of lower development; and so on, till the lifetime scenes of the fossil confronting him were a present and modern condition of things. These images passed before Knight's inner eye in less than half a minute, and he was again considering the actual present.

This elaborate evolutionary vision could have been sparked off by Leslie Stephen's brief snatch of geological observation in 'A Bad Five Minutes in the Alps': possibly Stephen's tendency to 'wild imaginings' while hanging on his cliff also influenced Hardy. But Knight's imaginings here are not 'wild' – they are a beautiful example of the scientific imagination engaged in 'retrospective prophecy' as described by Huxley.[27] The conjuring up of the entire evolutionary succession from one fossil parallels Huxley's imaginative journey into the past from the starting-point of one piece of chalk.[28] In Knight's time-journey, however, we could say that there are *two* starting-points, the other being Knight himself – the two ends of the evolutionary chain meet face to face. Man's 'mean' ancestry is brought home as an unpleasant truth that must be, literally, faced. Knight recognises his kinship with the trilobite, 'the single instance within reach of his vision of anything that had ever been alive and had had a body to save, as he himself had now'. On the one hand, Knight is the *same* as the trilobite – literally on the same level. But mentally he feels himself very different – the trilobite represents the 'mean' and 'small', lacking 'the dignity of man'; and later Hardy tells us that

Knight, without showing it much, knew that his intellect was above the average. And he thought – he could not help thinking – that his death would be a deliberate loss to earth of good material; that such an experiment in killing might have been practised upon some less developed life.

We have here a dramatisation of the two different, incompatible, ways that man relates to Nature in the scientific world view: by conscious, objective observation, and by physical, evolutionary kinship. Knight, as an objective, highly conscious, scientific observer, stares at the trilobite; but this observation brings home to him his kinship with such unconscious, primitive forms of life. Knight's position is in every way – physical and mental, literal and metaphorical – uncomfortable. There is an ironic parallelism between Knight's original 'experiment' on air-currents, and the idea that Nature is now practising experiments on him, the experimenter.

But despite the apparent hubris and nemesis pattern, Knight's qualities of objective observation and rational thought are not being devalued here: we feel he is right in his valuation of his intellect, and he rescues Elfride, who at first joins him in danger after a failed attempt to help him, by the exercise of the same quality that saved Leslie Stephen – enforced calm rationality:

He turned his eyes to the dizzy depths beneath them, and surveyed the position of affairs.

Two glances told him a tale with ghastly distinctness. It was that, unless they performed their feat of getting up the slope with the precision of machines, they were over the edge and whirling in mid-air.

For this purpose it was necessary that he should recover the breath and strength which his previous efforts had cost him. So still he waited, and looked in the face of the enemy. ...

'This piece of quartz, supporting my feet, is on the very nose of the cliff,' said Knight, breaking the silence after his rigid stoical meditation. 'Now what you are to do is this...'

and he succeeds at least in saving her, since the 'preternatural quiet and solemnity of his manner overspread herself, and gave her a courage not her own'. Suppression of emotion and retention of objective rationality are essential in dealings with Nature.

But, again like Leslie Stephen, Knight is not able to retain an objective viewpoint when left alone hanging on the cliff. The black cliff itself, like Stephen's black pinnacle, becomes a personal enemy: 'He looked far down the façade, and realised more thoroughly how it threatened him. Grimness was in every feature, and to its bowels the inimical shape was desolation.' More generally, he personifies the Nature that seems to be trying to destroy him, and slips into a more primitive, superstitious, frame of mind:

To those musing weather-beaten West-country folk who pass the greater part of their days and nights out of doors, Nature seems to have moods in other than a poetical sense: predilections for certain deeds at certain times, without any apparent law to govern or season to account for them. She is read as a person with a curious temper; as one who does not scatter kindnesses and cruelties alternately, impartially, and in order, but heartless severities or overwhelming generosities in lawless caprice. Man's case is always that of the prodigal's favourite or the miser's pensioner. In her unfriendly moments there seems a feline fun in her tricks, begotten by a foretaste of her pleasure in swallowing her victim.

Such a way of thinking had been absurd to Knight, but he began to adopt it now. He was first spitted on to a rock. New tortures followed. The rain increased, and persecuted him with an exceptional persistency which he was moved to believe owed its cause to the fact that he was in such a wretched state already. An entirely new order of things could be observed in this introduction of rain upon the scene. It rained upwards instead of down. The strong ascending air carried the rain-drops with it in its race up the escarpment... .

The wind, though not intense in other situations, was strong here. It tugged at his coat and lifted it. We are mostly accustomed to look upon all opposition which is not animate, as that of stolid, inexorable indifference, which wears out the patience more than the strength. Here at any rate, hostility did not assume that slow and sickening form. It was a cosmic agency, active, lashing, eager for conquest: determination; not an insensate standing in the way.

This is a confusing passage for the reader, as well as for Knight – as often with Hardy, there are strong effects pulling in contradictory directions. The first impression is that the 'weather-beaten West-country folk' have a truer insight into Nature's reality than the arrogant city-dweller Knight. What Knight previously dismissed as absurd, he is now forced to acknowledge. In this case, Hardy would be subscribing to a view of the Universe as subject to 'lawless caprice' – precisely the opposite of the vision of 'universal regular sequence, without partiality and without caprice'[29] presented by the scientific writers. Indeed, Hardy's words seem specially chosen to demolish the scientific world picture: Nature does not act 'impartially and in order', but with 'lawless caprice'. Presumably these words would have a startling effect on readers more accustomed to fervent declarations of belief in Nature's ordered, impartial structure. However, the passage about the West-country folk contains the strategic words 'seems' and 'apparent'. Nature *'seems* to have moods ... without any *apparent* law to govern or season to account for them', but the next paragraph makes clear that in this case, Knight's tortures are caused by the intelligible physical laws that govern the movements of air-currents – the very laws he began by expounding: 'The strong ascending air carried the rain-drops with it in its race up the escarpment.' Knight's feeling that the 'cause' is 'that he was in such a wretched state already' is plainly 'absurd'. It is Knight's enforced subjective perspective that causes his reversion to superstition, just as it is the fact that they have to live close to Nature that causes the beliefs of the West-country folk, who, in addition, do not know the underlying as opposed to apparent laws that cause Nature's behaviour. All this is quite in line with the scientific world view: Hardy is just exploiting the implication that there are other, less valid, more subjective, perspectives which produce other pictures, while at the same time reminding us of the objective reality from which they are deviating, in the same way that Leslie Stephen was able to offer us an objective and a subjective viewpoint on the same situation. Thus here, Hardy follows the personification of the actively hostile 'cosmic agency', with some detailed evidence of the distortion of Knight's sense of reality, of such objective facts as length of time, quantity, temperature, and colour:

'She will never come again; she has been gone ten minutes,' he said to himself.

This mistake arose from the unusual compression of his experiences just now: she had really been gone but three.... .

Next came another instance of the incapacity of the mind to make comparisons at such times.

'This is a summer afternoon,' he said, 'and there can never have been such a heavy and cold rain on a summer day in my life before.'

He was again mistaken. The rain was quite ordinary in quantity; the air in temperature. It was, as is usual, the menacing attitude in which they approached him that magnified their powers.

He then looks down at the sea: 'We colour according to our moods the objects we survey. The sea would have been a deep neutral blue, had happier auspices attended the gazer: it was now no otherwise than distinctly black to his vision.' The mistake about the time could have been suggested by the surprise with which Leslie Stephen discovers his ordeal has only lasted for five minutes.

But, despite these careful distinctions of subjective and objective, I still feel that a great deal of Hardy's sympathy lies with the world view of the West-country folk, and that he takes some ironic pleasure in making a scientific rationalist share it. Hardy's remark on a letter from Edward Clodd could cast some light here:

Mr E. Clodd this morning gives an excellently neat answer to my question why the superstitions of a remote Asiatic and a Dorset labourer are the same: 'The attitude of man', he says, 'at corresponding levels of culture, before like phenomena, is pretty much the same, your Dorset peasant representing the persistence of the barbaric idea which confuses persons and things, and founds wide generalisations on the slenderest analogies.'
  (This 'barbaric idea which confuses persons and things' is, by the way, also common to the highest imaginative genius – that of the poet.)[30]

In *A Pair of Blue Eyes*, Hardy does say that the folk idea of Nature is not 'poetical' – but I think he means here to stress that the view he is talking about is founded on practical experiences of real contact with Nature, not just poetical feelings about Nature. These real experiences are then expressed in terms of imaginative personifications. To the 'barbaric' rustic these personifications are not 'poetic', he really believes them – in fact, from his point of view they seem very probable hypotheses. Presumably Knight, if he were not an educated, scientific man who knows about air-currents, would come away from his experience on the cliff with such superstitious beliefs confirmed. But for him, as for Clodd, they are out-of-date superstitions that temporarily assault him: they are clearly of the same class as Leslie Stephen's 'wild imaginings'.

For Hardy as artist, however, the 'poetic' possibilities of such beliefs are very attractive, and he does not always keep up the clear distinction between what is produced by the subjective angle of the characters, and what is the 'objective' reality. For instance, even before the accident takes place, both Hardy as author and Elfride as another character, remark on the 'personality' of the cliff:

It is with cliffs and mountains as with persons; they have what is called a presence, which is not necessarily proportionate to their actual bulk. A little cliff will impress you powerfully; a great one not at all. It depends, as with man, upon the countenance of the cliff.

'I cannot bear to look at the cliff,' said Elfride. 'It has a horrid personality, and makes me shudder. We will go.'

Of course, Hardy could just be talking here about the general 'primitive' tendency of the human mind to anthropomorphise Nature. But a slight blurring between this tendency and the assertion of an objective fact is taking place. This is an inevitable danger of the re-introduction of what Tyndall calls 'ancient conceptions'[31] in a metaphorical or symbolic sense: once introduced, they can seem to take over if one does not keep painfully insisting that they are 'conscious and above board'. Thus, for instance, Hardy was annoyed to find people taking his phrase about 'the President of the Immortals' in *Tess of the D'Urbervilles* as an expression of a literal belief, rather than as the metaphorical personification that he had meant.[32] This sort of confusion seems to be produced by, as it were, pressing the Victorian scientific world picture at one of its weakest points, while still essentially remaining within it. Hardy often seems on the verge of deserting it entirely – for instance, in the passage about the 'West-country folk' he could almost be asserting a belief in Jungian 'synchronicity' – an acausal principle that connects events coincidentally in meaningful patterns. And in Knight's imaginings while on the cliff, Hardy could almost be embodying a belief in complete relativity – reality entirely depending on the subjective perspective of the observer. But in both cases, the insistent reminders of the objective facts and the physical laws that cause them, bring us back inside the world of Victorian science.

The tension, and sometimes confusion, between subjective and objective ways of seeing, the animistic and the scientific, synchronicity and natural causation, apparent during Knight's ordeal, has obvious parallels in Hardy's other novels – in their plot construction, and in the notorious 'inconsistencies' of the authorial commentary. Events are presented as, on the one hand, produced by an indifferent mechanism of causation, and on the other, as having a purposeful (usually malevolent) pattern. While it is sometimes clear that the pattern is only created by the subjectivity of those affected, or is only a metaphor of the author's, at other times this distinction is blurred. Yet the distinction is never completely done away with – we never enter a completely subjective and relative world.

But we have left Knight still hanging on the cliff. How is he to be rescued, and will the manner of his rescue suggest a way of escape from the philosophical and psychological tensions Hardy has subjected him to? If we were to look at his rescue with the eyes of D.H. Lawrence, this is what we might see: in the moment that Knight finally relaxes his conscious will he is rescued by Elfride, the embodiment of natural and instinctive life. But this is how Hardy puts it:

A fancy some people hold, when in a bitter mood, is that inexorable circumstance only tries to prevent what intelligence attempts. Renounce a desire for a long-contested position, and go on another tack, and after a while the prize is thrown at you, seemingly in disappointment that no more tantalizing is possible.

Knight gave up thoughts of life utterly and entirely and turned to contemplate the Dark Valley and the unknown future beyond. Into the shadowy depths of these speculations we will not follow him. Let it suffice to state what ensued.

At that moment of taking no more thought for this life, something disturbed the outline of the bank above him. A spot appeared. It was the head of Elfride.

Knight immediately prepared to welcome life again.

The idea that renunciation of conscious striving leads to a liberation is presented as only another subjective 'fancy'.

Moreover, it is a 'bitter' thought – like the whole experience on the cliff, this is another nasty trick that the Universe plays on conscious intelligence. Conscious intelligence is by no means devalued by the experience. And Knight's conscious intelligence is fully required to aid in the work of rescue. Elfride has impulsively removed all her underclothes to make a rope to save him:

> 'Now,' said Knight, who, watching the proceedings intently, had by this time not only grasped her scheme, but reasoned further on, 'I can hold three minutes longer yet. And do you use the time in testing the strength of the knots, one by one.'
> She at once obeyed, testing each singly by putting her foot on the rope between each knot, and pulling with her hands. One of the knots slipped.
> 'Oh, think! It would have broken but for your forethought,' Elfride exclaimed apprehensively.

These are not trivial points – part of the force of the whole passage comes from our intense involvement with conscious human intelligence battling skilfully and determinedly against natural forces. It is like watching the 'chess-game' with Nature that Huxley describes.[33] The co-operation in rescue between Knight and Elfride here might suggest a symbol of reconciliation between reason and instinct – but Hardy does not appear to want to bring out this application, and the subsequent history of their relationship suggests that all the tensions are still unresolved. The experience on the cliff is not finally educative for Knight – it merely dramatises the irreconcilables in his nature and condition.

If we take Hardy to be posing the same question as Leslie Stephen – 'What is this universe in which we live, and what is therefore the part we should play in it?' – we can conclude that he provides some more complicated answers, set in the same framework. The evolutionary passage in particular suggests that Hardy *is* leading us from the particular situation towards some such more general question. Like Stephen, Hardy sees agnostic man resolutely facing the destructive powers of inanimate Nature, and determinedly combatting them with his intelligence and will-power. In addition, Hardy seems to bring out some of the contradictions inherent in Stephen's world view. He dramatises the uncomfortable gap between the two ways Victorian science related man to Nature – conscious, intelligent observation, and evolutionary kinship to the most primitive, unconscious forms of life. He also exploits the idea that primitive, animistic ways of looking at the Universe can have a symbolic validity, and dramatises the resulting tension between objective and subjective ways of looking at the Universe. A possible parallelism is suggested here between man's primitive, subjective ways of thought, and man's evolutionary kinship to primitive Nature – both are contrasted with his highly developed, scientifically rational intelligence. Both are also presented as destructive, not life-giving: the trilobite, turned to stone now, is ultimately akin to the inanimate forces that try to kill Knight; and his subjective imaginings torture and confuse him. What is the part man should therefore play in such a tricky, contradictory Universe? The only faint sign of an answer is that he should use his conscious intelligence to save himself from the destructive forces once he has realised their power.

This sounds like a gradualist ideal, and we shall find it more fully developed in the way characters like Gabriel Oak relate to Nature in later novels. A question that might arise here is whether both Leslie Stephen and Hardy are not in fact setting up a Promethean model by chaining man to the cliff in this way. But in neither case could the ordeal on the cliff be said to be a punishment for limitless aspiration. Stephen seems rather to be willingly setting limits to his own freedom of thought and action. He renounces the unbounded speculations of theology, and tries out instead the perspective of a Prometheus bounded by natural laws. Hardy's Knight could be seen as aspiring to an impermissible objective detachment – but, as we have seen, the ordeal on the cliff appears more as a nasty trick than a just punishment. We do not feel that Knight was, like Frankenstein, meddling with or distorting Nature with a self-aggrandising purpose. It is rather uncontrolled Nature, in her 'experiment', who disturbs and inverts the harmonious order of his life: 'The world was to some extent turned upside down for him. Rain descended from below. Beneath his feet was aerial space and the unknown; above him was the firm, familiar ground, and upon it all that he loved best.'

It is interesting that in Hardy's other novels, it is often the most instinctive, 'natural', impulsive characters, such as Eustacia Vye in *The Return of the Native*, who create havoc and disorder, and who can be seen as Promethean aspirers, destroyed finally by the limits they did not recognise. As we have noticed in the cliff-hanging episode, the primitive is not life-giving, but destructive. For Hardy, as for Meredith, purely instinctive action is supremely inappropriate for conscious, civilised man – the behaviour that Nature demands is careful, conscious understanding. As I have suggested, Gabriel Oak in *Far From the Madding Crowd* exemplifies this type of behaviour towards Nature. I want to go on to illustrate in more detail the contrast between these two character types in some of Hardy's later novels. By this contrast, he seems to be separating out and developing more fully the two quite ways in which Victorian science related man to Nature, which conflict within one individual during Knight's ordeal on the cliff.

Gabriel Oak's objective, observant attitude to Nature is well illustrated by the way he notices the details (the toad on the path, the slug indoors) which give him foreknowledge of the impending storm, and lead to his attempt to save Bathsheba's ricks. Unlike Sergeant Troy, sunk in subjective drunkenness at this point, Oak understands the objective world, and how to deal with its often destructive forces. His intelligent working relationship with Nature is paralleled by Marty South and Giles Winterborne in *The Woodlanders*:

Marty South alone, of all the women in Hintock and the world, had approximated to Winterborne's level of intelligent intercourse with Nature ... to them the sights and sounds of night, winter, wind, storm, amid those dense boughs, which had to Grace a touch of the uncanny, and even of the supernatural, were simple occurrences whose origin, continuance and laws they foreknew.[34]

Like the scientists, and like Meredith's Melampus, Gabriel, Marty and Giles have an intelligent knowledge of underlying laws and causes that enables them to make predictions, and frees them from the 'figments of superstitious dread'.[35] It could of course be said that Oak is only exemplifying traditional country wisdom, the ancient craft of the shepherd, and his behaviour has nothing to do with the attitudes of 'modern' science. But if we compare the way he is described with the way Wordsworth, for instance, describes shepherds, we can see an important change of emphasis. Shepherds for Wordsworth are mysterious symbols of man's spiritual bond with his natural environment:

> aloft above my head,
> Emerging from the silvery vapours, lo!
> A Shepherd and his Dog! in open day:
> Girt round with mists they stood and look'd about
> From that enclosure small, inhabitants
> Of an aerial Island floating on,
> As seem'd, with that Abode in which they were,
> A little pendant area of grey rocks,
> By the soft wind breath'd forward.[36]

In 'Michael' we are given a less external portrayal of a shepherd, but it is the subjective impression made by his surroundings on his mind, till mind and Nature merge, that is emphasised:

> And grossly that man errs, who should suppose
> That the green valleys, and the streams and rocks,
> Were things indifferent to the Shepherd's thoughts.
> Fields, where with cheerful spirits he had breathed
> The common air; hills, which with vigorous step
> He had so often climbed; which had impressed
> So many incidents upon his mind
> Of hardship, skill or courage, joy or fear;
>
> . . . .
>
> Those fields, those hills – what could they less? had laid
> Strong hold on his affections, were to him
> A pleasurable feeling of blind love,
> The pleasure which there is in life itself.[37]

Specific details of 'skill' in objective, practical dealings with Nature – such as Gabriel's rescue of Bathsheba's bloated sheep – are omitted by Wordsworth. Conversely, Hardy stresses no particular subjective, emotional 'love' for Nature on Gabriel's part. Gabriel the shepherd, like the scientist Knight on the cliff, must stoically endure Nature's blows, and remain watchful, alert and unemotional in order to combat her worst destructions. It is this aspect of his shepherd's calling that Hardy has chosen to emphasise. To make another, more extreme, comparison, Gabriel is not either presented as an instinctual, sexual, 'natural' man, like D.H. Lawrence's gamekeeper Mellors, in *Lady Chatterley's Lover*. Interestingly, Hardy reserves this role for the rootless, impractical Sergeant Troy.

For Gabriel manages to retain objectivity towards his own emotions as well as towards Nature – unlike Farmer Boldwood he does not allow his unrequited love for Bathsheba to destroy him. We have seen in the passage from *A Pair of Blue Eyes* how these two areas, subjective emotion and Nature, were linked as primitive destructive forces by Hardy – Oak is able to control them both. Bathsheba reflects:

What a way Oak had, she thought, of enduring things. Boldwood, who seemed so much deeper and higher and stronger in feeling than Gabriel, had not yet learnt, any more than she herself, the simple lesson which Oak showed a mastery of by every turn and look he gave – that among the multitude of interests by which he was surrounded, those which affected his personal well-being were not the most absorbing and important in his eyes. Oak meditatively looked upon the horizon of circumstances without any special regard to his own standpoint in the midst.[38]

This is very like the 'objective' viewpoint advocated by George Eliot, and derived from the morality of science. Oak's quality of endurance is specifically linked with his non-Promethean acceptance of limiting circumstances – when he reappears after losing his sheep,

Gabriel was paler now. His eyes were more meditative, and his expression was more sad. He had passed through an ordeal of wretchedness which had given him more than it had taken away. He had sunk from his modest elevation as pastoral king into the very slime-pits of Siddim; but there was left to him a dignified calm he had never before known, and that indifference to fate which, though it often makes a villain of a man, is the basis of his sublimity when it does not.[39]

This quality of acceptance and adaptation is linked with a 'gradualist' rather than 'catastrophist' mode of being:

Oak's motions, though they had a quiet energy, were slow, and their deliberateness accorded well with his occupation. Fitness being the basis of beauty, nobody could have denied that his steady swings and turns in and about the flock had elements of grace. Yet, although if occasion demanded he could do or think a thing with as mercurial a dash as can the men of towns who are more to the manner born, his special power, morally, physically, and mentally, was static, owing little or nothing to momentum as a rule.[40]

A similar 'gradualism' appears in the behaviour of the reddleman in *The Return of the Native*, more explicitly mirroring and demanded by the 'gradualism' of Nature itself:

To do things musingly, and by small degrees, seemed, indeed, to be a duty in the Egdon valleys at this transitional hour, for there was that in the condition of the heath itself which resembled protracted and halting dubiousness. It was the quality of the repose appertaining to the scene. This was not the repose of actual stagnation, but the apparent repose of incredible slowness.[41]

Gabriel's 'static' nature is also not an unhealthy 'stagnation' – in this he is contrasted with Boldwood:

his was not an ordinary nature. That stillness, which struck casual observers more than anything else in his character and habit, and seemed so precisely like the rest of inanition, may have been the perfect balance of enormous antagonistic forces – positives and negatives in fine adjustment. His equilibrium disturbed, he was in extremity at once. If an emotion possessed him at all, it ruled him; a feeling not mastering him was entirely latent. Stagnant or rapid, it was never slow. He was always hit mortally or he was missed.[42]

Boldwood's is explicitly a 'catastrophist' psychology, given to sudden, explosive changes. Hardy's method of describing character in terms of physical forces – 'static', 'momentum', 'positives and negatives', 'equilibrium' – is reminiscent of the way Herbert Spencer often describes the operations of the mind in physical terms. For instance, in *First Principles*, Spencer states that

If we contemplate mental actions as extending over hours and days, we discover equilibrations analogous to those hourly and daily established among the bodily functions. In the one case as in the other, there are rhythms which exhibit a balancing of opposing forces at each extreme, and the maintenance of a certain general balance.[43]

Or in the *Principles of Psychology*, he defines 'the two antagonistic processes by which consciousness subsists – the centrifugal and centripetal actions by which its balance is maintained'.[44]

Sergeant Troy's character differs from the gradualist ideal in another way. He has no mental connection to past and future, existing in a permanent present of immediate impulse. Thus he is out of harmony with the gradual, connected processes of Nature; and he lacks the scientific objectivity that connects cause and effect, makes useful predictions, and achieves effective action:

He was a man to whom memories were an encumbrance, and anticipations a superfluity. Simply feeling, considering, and caring for what was before his eyes, he was vulnerable only in the present. His outlook upon time was as a transient flash of the eye now and then... .

Troy was full of activity, but his acties were less of locomotive than a vegetative nature; and, never being based upon any original choice of foundation or direction, they were exercised on whatever object chance might place in their way. Hence, whilst he sometimes reached the brilliant in speech because that was spontaneous, he fell below the commonplace in action, from inability to guide incipient effort. He had a quick comprehension and considerable force of character; but, being without the power to combine them, the comprehension became engaged with trivialities whilst waiting for the will to direct it, and the force wasted itself in useless grooves through unheeding the comprehension.

Bathsheba shows a similar dislocation of impulse and controlling reason, present feeling and future consequence: 'she felt her impulses to be pleasanter guides than her discretion... . Her culpability lay in her making no attempt to control feeling by subtle and careful inquiry into consequences.'[46] Here, we are reminded strongly of the scientific writers' morality of consequences, the objective vision of connected cause and effect that they felt should guide human conduct as well as scientific inquiry. As we have seen, Gabriel Oak possesses this guiding vision in his dealings both with external Nature and with his own emotions.

While Gabriel's conscious, rational, 'gradualist' approach puts him in harmony with Nature, in another sense it is Bathsheba and Troy who behave most 'naturally', in the sense of 'impulsively' or 'instinctively', even though Troy is an 'outsider', detached from the 'natural' world that Oak relates to. This paradox is explained if we remember once more the two different ways in which Victorian science related man to Nature – by a conscious, rational scientific understanding, and by an instinctual, physical evolutionary bond. Here Hardy embodies the rational in Gabriel, the instinctual in Bathsheba and Troy, particularly in their impulsive sexual attraction towards each other. For Hardy, sex is a potentially destructive primitive force, arising from our animal ancestry, our physical oneness with Nature. Curtis Webster has suggested that Hardy's early love poetry was influenced by Darwin's section on 'Sexual Selection' in *The Origin of Species*:

Love, as Hardy sees it, clearly depends on physical attraction. There is no rational cause for man's attraction to woman or woman's attraction to man. Sexual selection appears to operate much the same with human beings as with the species Darwin analysed... . Man, exercising his reason, would prefer that compatability should be the basis for love; Nature cares for neither man's wishes nor man's ethic and dictates that physical attraction should be the basis for mating.[47]

This is obviously also very true of Hardy's portrayal of sexual relationships in all his novels, and if we look in more detail at the passage from Darwin, an especial closeness to *Far from the Madding Crowd* emerges. Darwin remarks that

Generally, the most vigorous males, those which are best fitted for their places in nature, will leave the most progeny. But in many cases, victory depends not on general vigour, but on having special weapons, confined to the male sex. A hornless stag or spurless cock would have a poor chance of leaving offspring.[48]

He goes on to describe other varieties of competition among males to attract females – some birds 'display their gorgeous plumage and perform strange antics before the females, which standing by as spectators, at last choose the most attractive partner'.[49] One is irresistibly reminded of the strange incident in which Sergeant Troy demonstrates the sword-exercise to the fascinated Bathsheba. Troy, clad in his scarlet 'gorgeous plumage', performs 'strange antics' in front of his female 'spectator', as he shows off his 'special weapon'. Conforming to her natural instincts, Bathsheba is helplessly attracted to him – as Darwin puts it in *The Descent of Man*, 'The females are most excited by, or prefer pairing with, the more ornamented males, or those which are the best songsters, or play the best antics'.[50]

An important implication of Darwin's theory of sexual selection is that these sexually-attractive males need not necessarily be well-fitted for survival in other ways – they need not be 'those which are best fitted for their places in nature', if they can win the competition among the males for the females by means of special weapons or alluring appearance. Similarly, though Hardy presents Gabriel Oak and Giles Winterborne as the men best adapted to their natural surroundings in their respective novels, it is the more flashily attractive Sergeant Troy and Edred Fitzpiers who have more success in fascinating the women, though both these men are singularly out of harmony with their natural and social environmens. As we have seen, Troy as farmer is an incompetent anomaly; and Fitzpiers impresses Grace Melbury like this:

It was strange to her to come back from the world to Little Hintock and find in one of its nooks, like a tropical plant in a hedgerow, a nucleus of advanced ideas and practices which had nothing in common with the life around.[51]

These 'advanced ideas' have no practical value: 'the doctor was not a practical man, except by fits, and much preferred the ideal world to the real, and the discovery of principles to their application.'[52]

Tracing this pattern in *The Woodlanders*, we must not be confused by the fact that the impractical, impulsive Fitzpiers is presented as a 'scientist' – and a very Frankensteinian scientist at that. He conducts sinister anatomical experiments, he quotes Shelley, he compares himself to Prometheus.[52] But it is significant that Hardy explicitly denies the essential importance of science to Fitzpiers's character:

Fitzpiers was in a distinct degree scientific, being ready and zealous to interrogate all physical manifestations; but primarily he was an idealist. He believed that behind the imperfect lay the perfect; that rare things were to be discovered amidst a bulk of commonplace; that results in a new and untried case might be different from those in other cases where the material conditions had been precisely similar. Regarding his own personality as one of unlimited possibilities, because it was his own (notwithstanding that the factors of his life had worked out a sorry product for thousands), he saw a grand speciality in his discovery at Hintock of an altogether exceptional being of the other sex.[53]

Unlike Frankenstein, who expresses his Promethean sense of 'unlimited possibilities' through his science, Fitzpiers' Prometheanism is seen to be at odds with a scientific sense of the limits imposed by objective fact and the uniformity of nature. His role as scientist is a red herring, partly created by Grace's imagination: 'Miss Melbury's view of the doctor as a merciless, unwavering, irresistible scientist was not quite in accordance with fact'.[54] Though Hardy presents him as an exponent of 'advanced ideas', his Shelleyan dilettantism in fact seems rather outmoded, as if Hardy is making use of a well-worn stereotype, while the presentation of Giles' more 'primitive' 'intelligent intercourse with Nature', is, in literary terms, quite new.

Just as we could contrast Gabriel Oak's way of relating to Nature with that of Wordsworth's Michael, so here we can contrast Giles' practical 'sympathy' towards the trees he plants with the 'mental unity' that the Romantic Fitzpiers imagines he has with Nature: 'He dreamed and mused till his consciousness seemed to occupy the whole space of the woodland round, so little was there of jarring sight or sound to hinder perfect mental unity with the place.'[55] Of course, this is a travesty of the subtle inter-reactions of subjective and objective in Romantic Nature poetry – but it shows clearly the change of emphasis Hardy wants to bring about. Like the scientific writers, he sees dreamy subjectivity as the worst state of mind in which to approach Nature. Nature *should* 'jar' on our idealism – it contains many harsh realities that must be faced. This is what Fitzpiers should be seeing:

> Here, as everywhere, the Unfulfilled Intention, which makes life what it is, was as obvious as it could be among the depraved crowds of a city slum. The leaf was deformed, the curve was crippled, the taper was interrupted; the lichen ate the vigour of the stalk, and the ivy slowly strangled to death the promising sapling.[56]

Or this: 'Next were more trees close together, wrestling for existence, their branches disfigured with wounds resulting from their mutual rubbings and blows... . Beneath them were the rotting stumps of those of the group that had been vanquished long ago'.[57] Once again, we are being made to face Nature's harshness and imperfection.

These often-quoted 'Darwinian' passages are not just set-pieces: they provide the framework within which the characters act. Unlike Fitzpiers, Giles is not blind to Nature's imperfections, but he can also see beyond them to their 'origin, continuance and laws', and therefore he can take 'intelligent' action which will counteract the usual imperfections of the natural order:

> He had a marvellous power of making trees grow. Although he would seem to shovel in the earth quite carelessly there was a sort of sympathy between himself and the fir, oak, or beech that he was operating on; so that the roots took hold of the soil in a few days. When, on the other hand, any of the journeymen planted, although they seemed to go through an identically similar process, one quarter of the trees would die away during the ensuing August.[58]

This power of Giles' seems at first like the fulfilment of Fitzpiers' baseless, idealistic hope that 'results in a new and untried case might be different from those in other cases where the material conditions had been precisely similar'. But we soon learn Winterborne's magic is based on knowledge and forethought:

> Winterborne's fingers were endowed with a gentle conjurer's touch in spreading the roots of each little tree, resulting in a sort of caress under which

the delicate fibres all laid themselves out in their proper directions for growth. He put most of these roots towards the south-west; for, he said, in forty years time, when some great gale is blowing from that quarter, the trees will require the strongest holdfast on that side to stand against it and not fall.[59]

Winterborne is working in 'harmony' with Nature here, with a sympathetic understanding; but he is also working 'against' Nature by giving each individual tree a specially advantageous relationship to its environment, and so counteracting the destructive processes of the struggle for existence, which would usually ensure that a certain proportion of the trees would not survive. In Huxley's terminology, Winterborne is combatting the cosmic process (survival of the fittest), by the ethical process (the fitting of as many as possible to survive).[60] But such action can only be effective when based on a sympathetic understanding of the way the cosmic process works.

In contrast, Fitzpiers is blind to the realities of the cosmic process, not only in outer Nature but also in himself, and so can exercise no conscious control over it. Just as his subjective idealism prevented him from seeing the imperfections of the woodland, so it blinds him to the ordinary, and imperfect, natural processes of sexual selection that cause his feelings for Grace:

Regarding his own personality as one of limitless possibilities, because it was his own (notwithstanding that the factors of his life and worked out a sorry product for thousands), he saw a grand speciality in his discovery at Hintock of an altogether exceptional being of the other sex.[61]

So instead of thinking with but acting against the imperfect natural process, Fitzpiers acts out its imperfections in his disastrously impulsive sexual behaviour. The 'primitive' impulses that underlie his idealisations of the opposite sex are most clear in his pursuit and conquest of Suke Damson, which has an interesting Darwinian parallel in *The Descent of Man*. Darwin is moving from examples of sexual selection among animals, to examples of similar behaviour among primitive peoples:

With the Kalmucks there is a regular race between the bride and bridegroom, the former having a fair start; and Clarke 'was assured that no instance occurs of a girl being caught, unless she has a partiality to the pursuer'.[62]

(Suke finally gives away her hiding-place, and admits that she realised Fitzpiers was her pursuer.) The midsummer ritual that precedes the race, and that involves competition for Grace's 'capture' between Fitzpiers and Winterborne, (Winterborne, of course, loses), can be seen as a primitive sexual-selection procedure, from which Fitzpiers emerges with the greatest success.

So in the contrast between Fitzpiers and Winterborne we can see Hardy once again dramatising the two conflicting ways of relating to Nature that are implied in the Victorian scientific world view: by allowing ourselves to be controlled by the primitive and often destructive instincts we inherit from our animal ancestry; or by consciously understanding and controlling natural forces, in order to live in harmonious adaptation to them. Paradoxically, both ways can be called 'natural' – the first directly and unconsciously expresses the imperfect workings of Nature; the second consciously enacts man's 'natural' adaptation to his imperfect natural environment. This paradox is of course most prominent in *The Return of the Native*, where it is the subjective, impulsive, destructive, sexually fascinating Eustacia Vye who is most akin in character to her wild natural surroundings on Egdon Heath, while consciously she hates the heath, and finds it limiting and imprisoning. On the other hand, Clym Yeobright, the thoughtful, rational man, loves and identifies with the heath, and finds contentment working harmoniously with it as a furze-cutter. Significantly, Eustacia is surrounded with Promethean imagery; while Clym, if he is a Prometheus in his intellectual aspirations, is a Prometheus already fettered – 'As is usual with bright natures, the deity that lies chained within an ephemeral human carcase shone out of him like a ray.'[63]

Clym is explicitly presented as a modern agnostic, whose face mirrors the disillusionment that increases 'as we uncover the defects of natural laws, and see the quandary man is in by their operation'.[64] The 'uncovering' echoes once again Huxley's metaphor of stripping off Nature's religious disguise in order to reveal her 'uglier features'. The face of Nature thus revealed is well represented by the initial description of the heath, in which Clym's 'modern' sympathy with it is also prefigured:

It was a spot which returned upon the memory of those who loved it with an aspect of peculiar and kindly congruity... . The qualifications which frequently invest the façade of a prison with far more dignity than is found in the facade of a palace double its size lent to this heath a sublimity which spots renowned for beauty of the accepted kind are utterly wanting... . The time seems near, if it has not actually arrived, when the chastened sublimity of a moor, a sea, or a mountain will be all of nature that is absolutely in keeping with the moods of the more thinking among mankind.[65]

The substitution of prison for palace recalls Leslie Stephen's dismissal of 'a fanciful palace' as an appropriate image of the Universe; the 'prison' image by contrast appropriately evokes the harsh limitations that the new scientific picture of Nature imposed on man's aspirations. However, it is not often noticed that Egdon is two-sided. In contrast to its usual 'subdued' appearance, it also has a more violent side, that appeals not to grim agnostic rationality, but to subjective emotion, superstition and dreams:

during winter darkness, tempests and mists ... Egdon was roused to reciprocity; for the storm was its lover, and the wind its friend. Then it became the home of strange phantoms; and it was found to be the hitherto unrecognised original of those wild regions of obscurity which are vaguely felt to be compassing us about in midnight dreams of flight and disaster, and are never thought of after the dream till revived by scenes like this.[66]

This is clearly the aspect of Nature that Eustacia expresses in her behaviour. Human 'nature', as imaged in the heath, appears again as divided between two equally 'natural' but incompatible modes of behaviour. We can either learn to love our natural 'prison', and subdue our behaviour to its subdued 'monotony';[67] or we can court 'disaster' by giving ourselves over to a wild and destructive Nature, the 'home of strange phantoms', which is akin to, and perhaps produced by, our subconscious 'dreams', as much as the 'prison' image of Nature is produced by our conscious rationalist disillusionment.

In a sense, both aspects of Nature can be seen as comprised

within Clym's character, as they were within Knight's. Clym
does succumb to his disruptive feelings for Eustacia, as Knight
does to his for Elfride – Clym is not called upon to show the
stoic self-control of Gabriel Oak or Giles Winterborne. Clym's
scientific rationalism, and the way it is written on his thought-
worn face, provide further similarities with Knight. Bearing
these similarities in mind, we might want to see a parallelism
between the scene where Clym, working on the heath, becomes
identified with the insects around him, and Knight's similar
identification with the lowly trilobite, to which science has
shown he is akin. Here is Clym as seen by his mother:

She followed the figure indicated. He appeared of a russet hue, not more
distinguishable from the scene around him than the green caterpillar from the
leaf it feeds on.... . The silent being who thus occupied himself seemed to be of
no more account in life than an insect. He appeared as a mere parasite of the
heath, fretting its surface in his daily labour as a moth frets a garment, entirely
engrossed with its products, having no knowledge of anything in the world
but fern, furze, heath, lichens, and moss.[68]

The tone of horrified recognition of a demeaning kinship is
very similar to Knight's reaction to his trilobite ancestry. But
the scene from Clym's point of view has a different dimension:

His daily life was of a curious microscopic sort, his whole world being limited
to a circuit of a few feet from his person. His familiars were creeping and
winged things, and they seemed to enroll him in their band. Bees hummed
around his ears with an intimate air, and tugged at the heath and furze-
flowers at his side in such numbers as to weigh them down to the sod. The
strange amber-coloured butterflies which Egdon produced, and which were
never seen elsewhere, quivered in the breath of his lips, alighted upon his
bowed back, and sported with the glittering point of his hook as he flourished it
up and down. Tribes of emerald-green grasshoppers leaped over his feet, falling
awkwardly on their backs, heads, or hips, like unskilful acrobats, as chance might
rule; or engaged themselves in noisy flirtations under the fern-fronds with silent
ones of homely hue. Huge flies, ignorant of larders and wire-netting, and quite in
a savage state, buzzed about him without knowing that he was a man. In and out
of the fern-dells snakes glided in their most brilliant blue and yellow guise, it
being the season immediately following the shedding of their old skins, when
their colours are brightest. Litters of young rabbits came out from their forms to
sun themselves upon hillocks, the hot beams blazing through the delicate tissue of
each thin-fleshed ear, and firing it to a blood-red transparency in which the veins
could be seen. None of them feared him.

The monotony of his occupation soothed him, and was in itself a pleasure. A forced limitation of effort offered a justification of homely courses to an unambitious man, whose conscience would hardly have allowed him to remain in such obscurity while his powers were unimpeded. Hence Yeobright sometimes sang to himself.[69]

We have here the familiar anti-Promethean theme of a contented acceptance of limitation, as if Knight should come to enjoy the concentration of consciousness imposed by his limiting position on the cliff. But there is also a new theme – a more positive attitude to the idea of our kinship with the humbler forms of Nature, as if Knight should metaphorically 'let go' and find himself enjoying life among the trilobites. But of course these are not stony trilobites, they are lovingly described living insects, and Hardy builds up a sense of brotherhood through phrases such as 'enroll him in their band', 'an intimate air' and 'None of them feared him.' Interestingly, Clym has had to 'let go' of his more conscious, ambitious purposes in order to experience this brotherhood. We find a similar sense of physical oneness with Nature in the descriptions of Giles Winterborne in *The Woodlanders*, also of course linked with an occupation that puts him in harmony with Nature:

He looked and smelt like Autumn's very brother, his face being sunburnt to wheat-colour, his eyes blue as corn-flowers, his sleeves and leggings dyed with fruit-stains, his hands clammy with the sweet juice of apples, his hat sprinkled with pips, and everywhere about him that atmosphere of cider which at its first return each season has such an indescribable fascination for those who have been born and bred among the orchards.[70]

Giles' oneness with Nature becomes most complete when he is dying – it has been pointed out that Giles here 'moves down the evolutionary scale',[71] his cough sounding at first like 'a squirrel or a bird', and his delirious voice finally sounding like part of the inanimate world: 'an endless monologue, like that we sometimes hear from inanimate nature in deep secret places where water flows, or where ivy leaves flap against stones'.[72] This gentle dissolution into water is very different from Knight's precipitous plunge 'down the evolutionary scale' towards the destructive sea. As with Clym among the insects, Hardy is here expressing in a more positive way the scientific writers' sense of our physical kinship with the primitive and ultimately the inanimate. Nevertheless, he always shows this admission of physical oneness with Nature to involve a loss of conscious identity and purpose. Giles dies; Clym loses sight (literally – he is half blind) of his higher purposes – this limitatin may seem good to him; but his mother's disturbing vision of him is also valid, and implies he is less than human: 'a mere parasite of the heath ... entirely engrossed with its products, having no knowledge of anything in the world but fern, furze, heath, lichens, and moss'. Significantly, this more reductive perspective occurs *after* the passage that evokes Clym's sense of brotherhood.

So for Hardy, our organic relationship to the whole of Nature is in the end just one more limiting and reductive truth unveiled by science. We can find some joy in it, as we can come to love the grim, reduced beauty of the imprisoning heath. But there is no sense of a *progression* from a more reductive to a more organic vision of the Universe, as in Meredith's 'Meditation under Stars', where an acceptance of limitation leads on to a transforming vision of unity. For Hardy, the scientific fact of our physical bond to Nature does not expand into an overall coherent scientific vision of relationship and oneness, in which all the religious values lost by an acceptance of reductive truth can be rediscovered. Here we can see that he differs also from George Eliot. Such gleams as he shows of such a vision appear characteristically as detached, incongruous asides in his novels – like this, for instance, from *The Woodlanders*:

Hardly anything could be more isolated or more self-contained than the lives of these two walking here in the lonely hour before day, when grey shades, material and mental, are so very grey. And yet their lonely courses formed no detached design at all but were part of the pattern in the great web of human doings then weaving in both hemispheres from the White Sea to Cape Horn.[73]

But this insight is not allowed to enter and transform the consciousness of any of the characters, nor does the narrator use it to give coherence, pattern and meaning to the events, or to transform our view of them consistently. In *The Dynasts*, Hardy does, of course, try to provide a consistent structure based on such a vision of universal interconnection – but readers may rightly feel that his true genius lies in the dramatisation of incongruities, clashing perspectives, old and new viewpoints in unresolved conflict, that we find in his novels. What could be more incongruous, but also more powerful, as an embodiment of the paradoxical implications of Victorian science, than the vision of a scientific experimenter hanging half-way down a cliff in fear of his life, staring into the stony eyes of a fossilised trilobite?

Notes

Introdution

1 Stanza cxx, 5–8.
2 Thomas Carlyle, *Sartor Resartus* (Dent, 1973), p. 1.
3 Matthew Arnold, 'Literature and Science', *Discourses in America* (Macmillan, 1896), p. 112.
4 See esp. chs 3 and 4.
5 Alfred North Whitehead, *Science and the Modern World* (Cambridge, 1926), pp. 134, 138, 160.
6 Robert Langbaum 'The Dynamic Unity of *In Memoriam*', *The Modern Spirit* (Chatto & Windus, 1970), p. 51.
7 U.C. Knoepflmacher and G.B. Tennyson (eds) *Nature and the Victorian Imagination* (California UP, 1977), p. xix.
8 Lionel Stevenson, *Darwin Among the Poets* (New York, Russell & Russell, 1963), p. 7. See also Georg Roppen, *Evolution and Poetic Belief: A Study in Some Victorian and Modern Writers* (Oslo UP, 1956), p. 458.
9 T.H. Huxley, 'The Advisableness of Improving Natural Knowledge' (1866), *Collected Essays*, 9 vols (Macmillan, 1893–4), vol. 1; *Methods and Results*, pp. 30, 31, 41.
10 Edward Dowden, 'The Scientific Movement and Literature', *Studies in Literature, 1789–1877* (Kegan Paul, 1889), p. 89.
11 Leonard Huxley, *Life and Letters of Thomas Henry Huxley*, 2 vols (Macmillan, 1900), I, 9; II, 34, 268. John Tyndall, 'Personal Recollections of Thomas Carlyle' (1890), *New Fragments* (Longmans, 1892), pp. 348–52. A.S. Eve and C.H. Creasey, *The Life and Work of John Tyndall* (Macmillan, 1945), pp. 73–5. See also Frank M. Turner, 'Victorian Scientific Naturalism and Thomas Carlyle', *Victorian Studies*, 18 (March 1975), 325–43.
12 Culler, *The Poetry of Tennyson* (Yale UP, 1977), p. 15.
13 'The Scientific Movement and Literature', op. cit., pp. 112–3, 115.
14 ibid., pp. 113–14.
15 Stephen Prickett, *Victorian Fantasy* (Harvester, 1979), pp. xiii–xv.
16 Mary Shelley, *Frankenstein*, in *Three Gothic Novels* (Penguin, 1968), pp. 305–6.

17. John Keats, *Lamia*, part II, 237, 230.
18 *Frankenstein*, pp. 308–9, 307.
19 John Tyndall, 'On the Study of Physics' (1854), *Fragments of Science*, 7th edn, 2 vols (Longmans, 1889), pp. 292, 302.
20 Leslie Stephen and Frederick Pollock, (eds), *Lectures and Essays*, 2 vols (Macmillan, 1879), Introduction by F. Pollock, I, 36–7, quoting from unpublished 'notebook of Clifford's later [?1868–71] Cambridge time'.
21 'The Scientific Movement and Literature', p. 99.

1 The Values of Science

1 John Tyndall, 'The Belfast Address' (1874), *Fragments*, II, 194.
2 T.H. Huxley, 'The Geneology of Animals' (1869), *Collected Essays*, vol. II, *Darwiniana*, p. 110.
3 Edward Dowden, 'The Scientific Movement and Literature', *Studies in Literature, 1789–1877* (Kegan Paul, 1889) p. 99
4 Charles Darwin, *On the Origin of Species* (John Murray, 1859), pp. 485, 130, 109.
5 John Tyndall, 'The Scientific Use of the Imagination' (1870), *Fragments*, II, 127. See also Howard E. Gruber, *Darwin on Man, A Psychological Study of Scientific Creativity* (New York, Dutton, 1974), pp. 1–257, for an account of Darwin's creative thought processes.
6 John Tyndall, 'Professor Virchow and Evolution' (1879), *Fragments*, II, 383.
7 Introduction, p. 13.
8 ibid., p. 32.
9 John Tyndall, 'The Rev. James Martineau and the Belfast Address' (1875), *Fragments*, pp. 246–7.
10 John Tyndall, 'Apology for the Belfast Address' (1874), *Fragments*, II, 205.
11 T. H. Huxley, 'The Scientific Aspects of Positivism', *FR* n.s. 5 (June 1869), 653.
12 T. H. Huxley, Letter of 1860, *Life and Letters*, I, 220.
13 T. H. Huxley, 'The Advisableness of Improving Natural Knowledge', p. 41.
14 T. H. Huxley, 'Science and Morals' (1886), *Collected Essays*, vol. IX: *Evolution and Ethics*, p. 146.
15 Clifford, 'The Ethics of Belief' (1877), *Lectures and Essays*, II, 183.
16 T. H. Huxley, 'Autobiography', *Methods and Results*, p. 16.
17 Leslie Stephen, 'An Agnostic's Apology', *An Agnostic's Apology and Other Essays* (Smith, Elder & Co., 1893), p. 3.
18 John Tyndall, 'Study of Physics', p. 292; see also p. 8 above.

19 George Eliot, 'The Influence of Rationalism', *FR* n.s. 1 (15 May 1865), 55.

20 John Tyndall, 'Science and Man' (1877), *Fragments*, II, 337.

21 John Morley, 'Byron', *FR* n.s. 8 (December 1870), 667.

22 T. H. Huxley, 'Science and Morals', p. 146.

23 Clifford, *Lectures and Essays*, Introduction, pp. 29–30.

24 Edward Clodd, *The Story of Creation: A Plain Account of Evolution* (Longmans, 1888), pp. 221–2.

25 Dowden, 'The Scientific Movement and Literature', pp. 116, 117.

26 T. H. Huxley, 'A Liberal Education' (1868), *Collected Essays*, III, *Science and Education*, p. 302.

27 John Tyndall, 'Study of Physics', p. 302.

28 Edward Clodd, *Thomas Henry Huxley*, (Blackwoods, 1902), quoting, with minor inaccuracies, Huxley, 'On the Physical Basis of Life' (1868), *Methods and Results*, pp. 132, 131.

29 Clodd, *Huxley*, p. 132.

30 ibid., p. 134, quoting 'Scientific Use of the Imagination,' p. 131.

31 Dowden, 'The Scientific Movement and Literature', pp. 93, 100, quoting 'Speculation: A Discourse', delivered at South Place Chapel, 16 January 1876, p. 40.

32 Morley, 'Byron', pp. 668–9.

33 Dowden, 'The Scientific Movement and Literature', p. 97.

34 John Tyndall, 'An Address to Students' (1868), *Fragments*, II, 90.

35 John Tyndall, 'Belfast Address', p. 191.

36 Clodd, *Huxley*, pp. 128, 129.

37 T.H. Huxley, 'The Connection of the Biological Sciences with Medicine' (1881), *Science and Education*, p. 371.

38 John Tyndall, 'Martineau and the Belfast Address', p. 245.

39 John Tyndall, 'Science and Man', p. 340.

40 John Tyndall, 'Recollections of Carlyle', p. 385.

41 T.H. Huxley, 'Bishop Berkeley on the Metaphysics of Sensation' (1871), *Collected Essays*, vol. VI, *Hume: with Helps to the Study of Berkeley*, p. 285.

42 John Tyndall, *The Glaciers of the Alps*, (John Murray, 1860), p. 130.

43 John Tyndall, 'On the Constitution of the Universe' (1865), *Fragments*, I, 20.

44 John Tyndall, *Heat, Considered as a Mode of Motion* (Longmans, 1863), pp. 433–4.

45 Edward Clodd, *Story of Creation*, pp. 231–2.

46 T.H. Huxley, 'Evolution and Ethics' (1893), *Evolution and Ethics*, pp. 49–50.

47 A.N. Whitehead, *Science and Modern World* (Cambridge, 1926), pp. 160, 99, 102.

48 Clodd, *Story of Creation*, p. 223.
49 Clifford, 'Body and Mind' (1874), *Lectures and Essays*, II, 59.
50 Clifford, 'The Unseen Universe' (1875), *Lectures and Essays*, I, 231.
51 Dowden, 'The Scientific Movement and Literature', pp. 103, 111.
52 Tyndall, 'Miracles and Special Providences', *Fragments*, II, 31–2.
53 Stephen, 'What is Materialism?', *An Agnostic's Apology*, p. 167.
54 Tyndall, 'Scientific Use of the Imagination', p. 104.
55 Tyndall, 'Science and Man', p. 338.
56 Frederic Harrison, 'Mr. Lewes's Problems of Life and Mind', *FR* n.s. 16 (July 1874), 99, reviewing George Henry Lewes, *Problems of Life and Mind*, First Series: *The Foundations of a Creed*, vol. I (Trübner, 1874).
57 C.M. Bowra, *The Romantic Imagination* (Oxford, 1961), p. 271.
58 'Lewes's Problems', p. 98.
59 Huxley, 'Science and Morals', p. 131. Boscovich was Rudjer J. Boscovic, 1711–87, a natural philosopher from Yugoslavia.
60 Tyndall, 'Belfast Address', p. 208.
61 Frederick Pollock, Introduction to Clifford, *Lectures and Essays*, p. 1.
62 Tyndall, 'Scientific Use of Imagination', p. 103.
63 Tyndall, 'Matter and Force' (1876), *Fragments*, II, 56.
64 Tyndall, 'Scientific Use of Imagination', pp. 104–7.
65 Huxley, 'On the Method of Zadig' (1880), *Collected Essays*, vol. 4: *Science and Hebrew Tradition*, pp. 9, 6, 18.
66 Huxley, 'On a Piece of Chalk' (1868), *Collected Essays*, vol. VIII, *Discourses Biological and Geological*, pp. 1–36, 36.
67 Huxley, 'The Study of Zoology' (1861), *Discourses*, p. 215.
68 Tyndall, 'Apology for the Belfast Address', p. 208; and p. 27 above.
69 Tyndall, 'Scientific Use of the Imagination', p. 107.
70 Clifford, *Lectures and Essays*, Introduction, pp. 36–7, quoting from unpublished notebook.
71 Thomas Carlyle, *Sartor Resartus*, Ch. 8.
72 *Life and Letters*, I, 220.
73 Huxley, 'Autobiography', p. 16.
74 Huxley, 'Science and Morals', p. 146.
75 Tyndall, 'Recollections of Carlyle', p. 387.
76 Tyndall, 'Matter and Force', p. 66.
77 J.D.Y. Peel, *Herbert Spencer: The Evolution of a Sociologist* (Heinemann, 1971), pp. 112–30.
78 Tyndall, 'Vitality' (1865), *Fragments*, II, 52.
79 Tyndall, 'Belfast Address', p. 201.
80 Dowden, 'The Scientific Movement and Literature', pp. 119, 120.
81 Huxley, 'Science and Morals', pp. 122, 123.
82 Huxley, 'Scientific and Pseudo-Scientific Realism' (1887), *Collected Essays*, vol. V, *Science and Christian Tradition*, p. 62.

83 Tyndall, 'Belfast Address', p. 168.
84 Clifford, 'Right and Wrong: the Scientific Ground of their Distinction' (1875), *Lectures and Essays*, II, 162.
85 Tyndall, 'Science and Man', pp. 356, 357.
86 Tyndall, 'Virchow and Evolution', p. 374.
87 Huxley, 'The Evolution of Theology' (1886), *Science and Hebrew Tradition*, p. 372.
88 Huxley, 'Physical Basis of Life', p. 164.
89 Huxley, 'The Principles of Morals', *Hume with Berkeley*, p. 239, my italics.
90 Tyndall, 'Matter and Force', p. 73.
91 Charles Darwin, *The Descent of Man, and Selection in Relation to Sex* (rev. edn., Chicago and New York: Rand, McNally & Co., 1874; re-published Gale Research Co., Detroit, 1974), pp. 116–17, 605.
92 Charles Darwin, *The Expression of the Emotions, in Man and Animals* (John Murray, 1872), chs. 5–14.
93 Clodd, *Huxley*, p. 204.
94 Herbert Spencer, *The Principles of Psychology*, 2nd edn., 2 vols (Williams & Norgate, 1870), I, 470–1.
95 Peel, *Herbert Spencer*, p. 120.
96 Darwin, *Descent of Man*, p. 124, quoting Alfred Russel Wallace, 'The Origin of Human Races Deduced from the Theory of Natural Selection', *Anthropological Review*, (May 1864), clviii.
97 ibid., p. 162.
98 Huxley, *Evolution and Ethics*, p. 82.
99 Huxley, 'Scientific Realism', p. 62; see also p. 34 above.

2 Tennyson

1 T. H. Huxley, *Life and Letters*, II, 337.
2 Hallam Tennyson, *Alfred, Lord Tennyson; A Memoir by his Son*, 2 vols (Macmillan, 1897), II, 475.
3 Edward Dowden, 'The Scientific Movement and Literature', pp. 112–13; see also p. 4 above.
4 Culler, *The Poetry of Tennyson*, p. 146; Basil Willey, *More Nineteenth-Century Studies* (Cambridge, 1980), pp. 101–3.
5 Hallam Tennyson, *Memoir*, II, 469.
6 Stevenson, *Darwin Among the Poets*, p. 95; Joseph Warren Beach, *The Concept of Nature in Nineteenth Century English Poetry* (New York, Russell & Russell, 1966), p. 432; Roppen, *Evolution and Poetic Belief*, p. 98.

 7 *Memoir*, I, 323.
 8 ibid.
 9 ibid., II, 380.
10 *The Poems of Tennyson*, ed. Christopher Ricks (Longmans, 1969), head-note to 'De Profundis', p. 1281. All my quotations from Tennyson's poems are from this edition.
11 John Tyndall, 'Scientific Use of the Imagination', p. 131; 'An Address to Students', p. 90; 'Martineau and the Belfast Address', p. 245. See also pp. 19–21 above.
12 John Tyndall, *Heat*, p. 433. See also p. 22 above.
13 John Tyndall, 'Vitality', p. 52.
14 John Tyndall, 'Belfast Address', p. 201.
15 John Tyndall, 'Science and Morals', p. 122; 'Scientific Realism', p. 62.
16 See Susan Gliserman, 'Early Victorian science writers and Tennyson's "In Memoriam": A study of cultural exchange', part I, *VS* 18 (March 1975): 277–308; G. Glen Wickens, 'The two sides of early Victorian science and the unity of "The Princess" ', *VS* 23 (March 1980), 369–88.
17 This is Wickens' argument.
18 Gliserman, op. cit., p. 287.
19 ibid., p. 292.
20 Culler, op. cit., p. 150.
21 Tyndall 'Study of Physics', p. 302.
22 Dowden, 'The Scientific Movement and Literature', p. 114.
23 See p. 94 below.
24 *Lectures and Essays*, I, 36-7; see also p. 31 above.
25 'Science and Morals', p. 146; see also p. 32 above.
26 Tyndall, 'Matter and Force', p. 56.
27 'The Influence of Rationalism', p. 55; see also p. 15 above.
28 Tyndall, 'On the Constitution of the Universe', p. 20.
29 Tyndall, *Heat*, pp. 433–4.
30 'Evolution and Ethics', pp. 44–50.
31 Darwin, *Origin*, p. 130; see also p. 12 above.
32 See Beach, *The Concept of Nature*, pp. 406–34, and Roppen, *Evolution and Poetic Belief*, pp. 66–112, esp. pp. 80, 82–3, 89, 91, 94.
33 John Killham, in *Tennyson and 'The Princess'* (Athlone Press, 1958), p. 246, points out that Tennyson is inconsistently bringing in the 'cataclysmic theory' here, and thus is 'not unwilling to keep in his mind three ultimately exclusive theories – the cataclysmic, the uniformitarian (Lyell's) and the quasi-evolutionary' (p. 250). But Tennyson's use of the word 'seeming' here gives the 'cataclysmic' a lesser reality, and allows it to be subsumed as a part of the uniformitarian / evolutionary blend he creates.
34 Clifford 'Body and Mind', p. 59.
35 See p. 59 above.

36 See Culler, *The Poetry of Tennyson*, pp. 167–8, for contemporary sources and analogues for the extension of scientific and evolutionary ideas to the concept of immortality.
37 Edward Dowden, 'Mr. Tennyson and Mr. Browning: A Comparative Study', *Studies in Literature*, p. 196.
38 Tennyson, *Poems*, p. 946, fn.
39 Willey, *More Nineteenth Century Studies*, p. 81.
40 See p. 14 above.
41 Hallam Tennyson, *Memoir*, I, 278.
42 See, e.g., stanzas XXXV, XCII.
43 See p. 28 above.
44 Dowden, 'The Scientific Movement and Literature', p. 112.
45 ibid., p. 114.

3 George Eliot

1 J.W. Cross, *George Eliot's Life* (New York, AMS Press, 1965), p. 426, 'Notes on the Spanish Gipsy'.
2 See *The George Eliot – George Henry Lewes Library: An Annotated Catalogue of their Books at Dr. Williams's Library, London* (Garland Publishing Inc., 1977), pp. 40, 49, 101, 203.
3 Gordon S. Haight, *George Eliot, A Biography* (Clarendon Press, 1968), p. 389.
4 G.W. Cooke, *George Eliot – A Critical Study of her Life, Writings and Philosophy* (Sampson Low, Marston, Searle & Rivington, 1883), ch. IX, 'Philosophic Attitude', p. 166.
5 Gordon S. Haight, (ed.) *The George Eliot Letters*, 7 vols (Oxford, 1954–6), V, 168-9.
6 *Middlemarch* (1872; Penguin, 1965), p. 226.
7 ibid., p. 122.
8 ibid., pp. 178, 790-1, 109.
9 ibid., p. 532.
10 ibid., p. 663
11 ibid., p. 178.
12 Mary Shelley, *Frankenstein*, (1818; Penguin 1968) pp. 306, 314.
13 *Middlemarch*, pp. 177-8.
14 For some illuminating analysis of this parallelism see David Carroll, '*Middlemarch* and the Externality of Fact', *This Particular Web: Essays on Middlemarch*, ed. Ian Adam (Toronto UP, 1975), p. 85; and 'Unity through Analogy: An Interpretation of *Middlemarch*', *VS* 2 (June 1959), 311.

15 Shelley, *Frankenstein*, p. 316.
16 *Middlemarch*, pp. 193-4.
17 T.H. Huxley, 'Natural Knowledge', pp. 40-1.
18 John Tyndall, 'Scientific Use of the Imagination', p. 127; see also p. 12 above.
19 John Tyndall, 'Miracles and Special Providences', pp. 31-2; see also pp. 27–28 above.
20 Tyndall, 'Scientific Use of the Imagination', p. 103; 'Matter and Force', p. 56; 'Apology for the Belfast Address', p. 208.
21 *Middlemarch*, p. 636.
22 ibid., p. 195.
23 John Tyndall, 'Study of Physics', p. 292; see also p. 8 above.
24 *Middlemarch*, p. 711.
25 ibid., p. 827.
26 ibid., p. 666.
27 ibid., pp. 757-8.
28 T.H. Huxley, 'Science and Morals', p. 146; see also p. 16 above.
29 *Middlemarch*, p. 46.
30 ibid., p. 520.
31 ibid., p. 178.
32 *Adam Bede* (1859; Penguin, 1980), pp. 148-9, 241. *The Mill on the Floss* (1860; Penguin, 1979), pp. 362-6.
33 *Middlemarch*, pp. 112, 225.
34 John Tyndall, 'Matter and Force', p. 56.
35 *Middlemarch*, pp. 66-7.
36 Huxley, 'Natural Knowledge', p. 41; Tyndall, 'Study of Physics', p. 212. See also pp. 14, 8 above.
37 *Middlemarch*, pp. 845-6.
38 See, e.g., Michael Mason, '*Middlemarch* and science: Problems of life and mind', *RES* n.s. 22 (May 1971), 168.
39 Tyndall, 'Scientific Use of the Imagination', p. 104; see also p. 26 above.
40 *Middlemarch*, p. 194.
41 ibid., pp. 83, 31-2, 194.
42 ibid., p. 177.
43 ibid., p. 170.
44 ibid., p. 177.
45 ibid., p. 210.
46 *Mill on the Floss*, pp. 590, 597, 601-2, 648, 94.
47 *Daniel Deronda* (1876; Penguin, 1967), pp. 526, 605-6.
48 ibid., pp. 587-8.
49 ibid., p. 787.
50 Edward Dowden, 'The Scientific Movement and Literature', pp. 103, 111.

51 *Daniel Deronda*, p. 593.
52 *Middlemarch*, pp. 175, 438.
53 ibid., p. 283.
54 Clifford, 'The Unseen Universe', p. 231.
55 *Middlemarch*, p. 896.
56 ibid.
57 ibid., p. 26.

4 Meredith

1 C. L. Cline (ed.), *The Letters of George Meredith*, 3 vols (Clarendon Press, 1970), I, 165, referring to Richard Owen, anatomist, 1804–92.
2 See *The Times*, 4 October 1862, p. 7.
3 ibid., p. 7.
4 Cline (ed.), *Letters*, I, 493.
5 ibid., p. 161.
6 See pp. 25, 14 above.
7 *Letters*, II, 843; III, 1443.
8 Edward Clodd, *Thomas Henry Huxley*, (Blackwoods, 1902), p. 211.
9 Cline (ed.), *Letters*, I, 279, 282, 288, 363 and note; II, 1072.
10 *FR*, n.s. 32 (October 1882), 519.
11 Cline (ed.), *Letters*, I, 326.
12 Edwin Everett, *The Party of Humanity* (Chapel Hill, North Carolina UP, 1939), p. 106.
13 All references to Meredith's poems are to *The Poetical Works of George Meredith*, ed. G.M. Trevelyan (Constable, 1912).
14 See Stevenson, *Darwin Among the Poets*, p. 212.
15 See pp. 31–35 above.
16 W.K. Clifford, *Lectures and Essays*, 2 vols (Macmillan, 1879), I, 36–7.
17 'The Influence upon Morality of A Decline in Religious Belief' (1877), *Lectures and Essays*, II, 248.
18 ibid., p. 247.
19 J. Cotter Morison, 'The Significance of Ritualism', *FR* n.s. 1 (January 1867), 75.
20 John Tyndall 'Miracles and Special Providences', pp. 31–2.
21 Charles Darwin, *Origin of Species*, (John Murray, 1859), pp. 186–7.
22 Clifford, 'On the Aims and Instruments of Scientific Thought' (1872), *Lectures and Essays*, I, 156.
23 Tyndall, 'Matter and Force', p. 73.
24 Tyndall, 'Martineau and the Belfast Address', pp. 246–7.
25 Cline (ed.), *Letters*, II, 841 (1886).

26 Darwin, op. cit., p. 130; see also p. 12 above.
27 Tyndall, 'Matter and Force', p. 56.
28 Tyndall, 'Constitution of the Universe', p. 20.
29 T.H. Huxley, 'Biological Sciences and Medicine', p. 371.
30 Dowden, 'Scientific Movement and Literature', pp. 97, 99.
31 Huxley, 'Evolution and Ethics', pp. 49–50.
32 Tyndall, 'Scientific Use of the Imagination', p. 131.
33 Tyndall, 'Constitution of the Universe', p. 20.
34 Huxley, 'Bishop Berkeley', p. 285.
35 Tyndall, 'Study of Physics', p. 302.
36 Tyndall, 'Matter and Force', p. 66.
37 John Morley, 'Byron', p. 666.
38 ibid., p. 667.
39 John Morley, 'Mr. Mill's Autobiography', *FR* n.s. 15 (January 1874), 16.
40 For an illuminating account of Darwin's relationship with Nature, see John Angus Campbell, 'Nature, religion and emotional response: A reconsideration of Darwin's affective decline', *VS* 18 (December 1974), 159–74.
41 See pp. 36–38 above.
42 See verses 11 and 12.

5 Hardy

1 J.W. Beach, *The Concept of Nature in Nineteenth-Century English Poetry*, (New York, Russell & Russell, 1966), p. 16.
 2 Florence Emily Hardy, *The Life of Thomas Hardy 1840–1928* (Macmillan, 1962), pp. 122, 153, 205.
 3 Harvey Curtis Webster, *On a Darkling Plain* (Archon Books, 1964), pp. 27, 34, 40–2, 45.
 4 F.E. Hardy, *Life*, pp. 230, 264, 100.
 5 Noel Annan, *Leslie Stephen: His Thought and Character in Relation to his Time* (Harvard UP, 1952), pp. 90–1.
 6 Leslie Stephen, *An Agnostic's Apology and Other Essays* (Smith, Elder & Co., 1893), pp. 3, 167; see also pp. 15, 25 above.
 7 *The Complete Poems of Thomas Hardy*, ed. James Gibson (Macmillan, 1978), pp. 111, 113.
 8 T.H. Huxley, 'Autobiography', p. 16; see also p. 15 above.
 9 Clifford, *Lectures and Essays*, I, 36–7; see also p. 31 above.
10 H.C. Webster, *On a Darkling Plain*, (Archon Books, 1964), pp. 42–4, 49–52.
11 F.E. Hardy, *Life*, p. 383.

12 Thomas Hardy, *Complete Poems*, p. 557.
13 ibid., pp. 116, 117, 118.
14 ibid., pp. 116, 111.
15 *A Pair of Blue Eyes* (Macmillan, 1975), chs. 21, 22.
16 Leslie Stephen, 'A Bad Five Minutes in the Alps', *Essays in Freethinking and Plainspeaking* (Longmans, 1853), ch. 5.
17 Robert Gittings, *Young Thomas Hardy* (Penguin, 1978), pp. 265–6.
18 Stephen, 'A Bad Five Minutes', pp. 155–60, 167, 178, 179, 175, 180, 172, 194–5, 165.
19 ibid., pp. 163, ibid., 166, 167, 171, 172.
20 John Tyndall, 'Science and Man', p. 357; see also p. 34 above.
21 Stephen, pp. 165–6, 172.
22 ibid., pp. 195–7, 172–3, 197.
23 *A Pair of Blue Eyes*, ch. 13, pp. 158–60.
24 Gittings, op. cit., p. 237.
25 Chs. 21–2, pp. 230–48. All subsequent quotations from *A Pair of Blue Eyes* are from these pages.
26 John Tyndall, *Glaciers*, p. 183.
27 T.H. Huxley, 'On the Method of Zadig', pp. 9, 6, 18; see also p. 28 above. A possible source for Knight's evolutionary vision has been suggested by Patricia Ingham, in 'Hardy and *The Wonders of Geology*', *RES* n.s. 31 (February 1980), 59–63. She finds a similar 'Retrospect' in a book that Hardy owned, called *The Wonders of Geology* (1838) by Gideon Algernon Mantell.
28 T.H. Huxley, 'On a Piece of Chalk'; see also p. 29 above.
29 George Eliot, 'The Influence of Rationalism', p. 55; see also p. 15 above.
30 F.E. Hardy, *Life*, p. 230.
31 John Tyndall, 'Science and Man', p. 357; see also p. 34 above.
32 F.E. Hardy, *Life*, p. 244.
33 T.H. Huxley, 'A Liberal Education', p. 82; see also p. 17 above.
34 *The Woodlanders* (1887) (Macmillan, 1974), pp. 357–8.
35 John Tyndall, 'Miracles and Special Providences', pp. 31–2; see also p. 25 above.
36 William Wordsworth, *Prelude* (1805), book 8, 93–101.
37 William Wordsworth, 'Michael', 62–77.
38 *Far From the Madding Crowd* (1874) (Macmillan, 1969), p. 328.
39 ibid., p. 49.
40 ibid., p. 18.
41 *The Return of the Native* (1878, Macmillan, 1968), p. 19.
42 *Far From the Madding Crowd*, p. 138.
43 Herbert Spencer, *First Principles* (Williams & Norgate, 1862), pp. 461–2.
44 Herbert Spencer, *The Principles of Psychology* (Longmans, 1855), p. 333. Other possible influences behind this way of describing character are the

French Utopian socialist, François Marie Fourier (see *The Literary Notes of Thomas Hardy*, ed. Lennart, A. Björk, 2 vols (Gothenburg Studies in English, 29, 1976), entry 1 in vol. 1: *Text*, and vol. 2, *Notes*); and the positivist, Auguste Comte (see *Literary Notes*, entries 727–8, in both vols).

45 *Far From the Madding Crowd*, p. 187.
46 ibid., p. 212.
47 Webster, *On a Darkling Plain*, pp. 68–70.
48 Charles Darwin, *Origin of Species*, p. 88.
49 ibid., p. 89.
50 Charles Darwin, *The Descent of Man*, p. 210. *The Descent of Man* contained an even longer section on sexual selection than *The Origin of Species* – indeed, its full title is *The Descent of Man and Selection in Relation to Sex*. Curtis Webster rejects *The Descent* as an influence on the early poems he discusses as it was not published until 1871, but obviously it could have influenced Hardy's novels written after this date, if only in confirming an already established attitude to sexual relationships.
51 *The Woodlanders*, pp. 80–1.
52 ibid., p. 144.
53 ibid., p. 164.
54 ibid., p. 153.
55 ibid., p. 170.
56 ibid., p. 83.
57 ibid., p. 339.
58 ibid., pp. 93–4.
59 ibid., p. 94.
60 T.H. Huxley, 'Prolegomena' to 'Evolution and Ethics', p. 82; see also p. 38 above.
61 *Woodlanders*, p. 164.
62 Darwin, *The Descent of Man*, pp. 592–3.
63 *Return of the Native*, p. 145.
64 ibid., p. 174.
65 ibid., pp. 12–13.
66 ibid., p. 13.
67 ibid.
68 ibid., p. 283.
69 ibid., pp. 258–9.
70 *The Woodlanders*, p. 340.
71 David Lodge, Introduction, *The Woodlanders*, p. 24.
72 *The Woodlanders*, p. 340.
73 ibid., p. 52.

Short Bibliography

Annan, Noel, *Leslie Stephen*, (Harvard UP, 1952).

Beach, Joseph Warren, *The Concept of Nature in Nineteenth-Century English Poetry* (New York, Russell & Russell, 1966).

Bowra, C.M., *The Romantic Imagination* (Oxford, 1961).

Campbell, John Angus, 'Nature, religion and emotional response: A reconsideration of Darwin's affective decline', *Victorian Studies* 18 (December 1974).

Carlyle, Thomas, *Sartor Resartus* (Dent, 1973).

Carroll, David, 'Unity Through Analogy' *VS* 2 (June 1959).

Carroll, David, '*Middlemarch* and the externality of fact', *This Particular Web*, ed. Ian Adam (Toronto UP, 1975).

Clifford, William Kingdon, *Lectures and Essays*, Leslie Stephen and Frederick Pollock (eds.), 2 vols (Macmillan, 1879).

Clodd, Edward, *The Story of Creation* (Longmans, 1888).

Clodd, Edward, *Thomas Henry Huxley* (Blackwoods, 1902).

Cooke, George Willis, *George Eliot* (Sampson Low, Marston, Searle & Rivington, 1883).

Cross, J.W., *George Eliot's Life* (New York, AMS Press, 1965).

Culler, A. Dwight, *The Poetry of Tennyson* (Yale UP, 1977).

Darwin, Charles, *On the Origin of Species* (John Murray, 1859).

Darwin, Charles, *The Descent of Man* (Chicago and New York, Rand, McNally, 1874; republished Gale Research Co., Detroit, 1974).

Darwin, Charles, *The Expression of the Emotions* (John Murray, 1874).

Dowden, Edward, *Studies in Literature, 1789–1877* (Keegan Paul, 1889).

Eliot, George, *Adam Bede* (Penguin, 1980).

Eliot, George, *Daniel Deronda* (Penguin, 1967).

Eliot, George, *The George Eliot Letters*, ed. Gordon S. Haight, 7 vols (Oxford, 1954–6).

Eliot, George, *The George Eliot – George Henry Lewes Library* (Garland Publishing Inc., 1977).

Eliot, George, *Middlemarch* (Penguin, 1965).

Eliot, George, *The Mill on the Floss* (Penguin, 1979).

Eve, A.S., and Creasey, C.H., *The Life and Work of John Tyndall* (Macmillan, 1945).

Everett, Edwin, *The Party of Humanity* (Chapel Hill, North Carolina UP, 1970).

Gliserman, Susan, 'Early Victorian science writers and Tennyson's "In Memorium"', part I, *VS* 18 (March 1975).

Gittings, Robert, *Young Thomas Hardy* (Penguin, 1978).

Gruber, Howard E., *Darwin on Man* (New York, Dutton, 1974).

Hardy, Florence Emily, *The Life of Thomas Hardy*, (Macmillan, 1962)

Hardy, Thomas, *The Complete Poems of Thomas Hardy*, ed. James Gibson (Macmillan, 1978).

Hardy, Thomas, *Far from the Madding Crowd* (Macmillan, 1974).

Hardy, Thomas, *The Literary Notes of Thomas Hardy*, ed. Lennart A. Björk (Gothenburg Studies in English, 29, 1976).

Hardy, Thomas, *A Pair of Blue Eyes* (Macmillan, 1975).

Hardy, Thomas, *The Return of the Native* (Macmillan, 1968).

Hardy, Thomas, *The Woodlanders* (Macmillan, 1974).

Harrison, Frederic, 'Mr. Lewes's problems of life and mind', *FR* n.s. 16 (July 1874).

Huxley, Leonard, *Life and Letters of Thomas Henry Huxley*, 2 vols (Macmillan, 1903).

Huxley, Thomas Henry, *Collected Essays*, 9 vols (Macmillan, 1893–4).

Ingham, Patricia, 'Hardy and *The Wonders of Geology*', *RES* n.s. 31 (February 1980).

Killham, John, *Tennyson and 'The Princess'* (Athlone Press, 1958).

Knoepflmacher, U.C., and Tennyson, G.B. (eds.), *Nature and the Victorian Imagination* (California UP, 1977).

Langbaum, Robert, *The Modern Spirit* (Chatto & Windus, 1970).

Lewes, George Henry, *Problems of Life and Mind*, first series, *The Foundations of a Creed* (Trübner, 1874).

Mason, Michael, '*Middlemarch* and science: Problems of life and mind', *RES* n.s. 22 (May 1971).

Meredith, George, *The Poetical Works of George Meredith*, ed. G.M. Trevelyan (Constable, 1912).

Meredith, George, *The Letters of George Meredith*, ed. C.L. Cline, 3 vols (Oxford, 1970).

Morison, J. Cotter, 'The significance of ritualism', *FR* n.s. 1 (January 1867).

Morley, John, 'Byron', *FR* n.s. 8 (December 1870).

Morley, John, 'Mr Mill's Autobiography', *FR* n.s. 15 (January 1874).

Peel, J.D.Y., *Herbert Spencer, The Evolution of a Sociologist* (Heinemann, 1971).

Prickett, Stephen, *Victorian Fantasy* (Harvester, 1979).

Roppen, Georg, *Evolution and Poetic Belief* (Oslo UP, 1956).

Shelley, Mary, *Frankenstein, Three Gothic Novels* (1818; Penguin, 1968).

Spencer, Herbert, *The Principles of Psychology* (Longmans, 1855).

Spencer, Herbert, *The Principles of Psychology* 2nd edn., 2 vols (Williams & Norgate, 1870).

Spencer, Herbert, *First Principles* (Williams & Norgate, 1862).

Stephen, Leslie, *Essays in Freethinking and Plainspeaking* (Longmans, 1853).

Stephen, Leslie, *An Agnostic's Apology and Other Essays* (Smith, Elder & Co., 1893).

Stevenson, Lionel, *Darwin Among the Poets* (New York, Russell & Russell, 1963).

Tennyson, Alfred, *The Poems of Tennyson*, ed. Christopher Ricks (Longmans, 1969).

Tennyson, Hallam, *Alfred, Lord Tennyson; a Memoir by his Son*, 2 vols (Macmillan, 1897).

Turner, Frank M., 'Victorian scientific naturalism and Thomas Carlyle', *VS* 18 (March, 1975).

Tyndall, John, *The Glaciers of the Alps* (John Murray, 1860).

Tyndall, John, *Heat, Considered as a Mode of Motion* (Longmans, 1863).

Tyndall, John, *Fragments of Science*, 7th ed., 2 vols (Macmillan, 1889).

Tyndall, John, *New Fragments* (Longmans, 1892).

Webster, Harvey Curtis, *On a Darkling Plain* (Archon Books, 1964).

Whitehead, Alfred North, *Science and the Modern World* (Cambridge, 1926).

Wickens, G. Glen, 'The two sides of early Victorian science and the unity of "The Princess"', *VS* 23 (March 1980).

Willey, Basil, *More Nineteenth Century Studies* (Cambridge, 1980).

Index